BEYOND BLESSED
STUDY GUIDE

BEYOND BLESSED STUDY GUIDE

GOD'S PERFECT PLAN TO OVERCOME ALL FINANCIAL STRESS

ROBERT MORRIS

Faith
Words

NEW YORK   NASHVILLE

FaithWords
Hachette Book Group
1290 Avenue of the Americas, New York, NY 10104
faithwords.com
twitter.com/faithwords

First Edition: February 2019

FaithWords is a division of Hachette Book Group, Inc. The FaithWords name and
logo are trademarks of Hachette Book Group, Inc.

The publisher is not responsible for websites (or their content)
that are not owned by the publisher.

The Hachette Speakers Bureau provides a wide range of authors for speaking events.
To find out more, go to www.hachettespeakersbureau.com or call (866) 376-6591.

ISBN: 978-1-5460-1011-1

Printed in the United States of America

LSC-C

10 9 8 7 6 5 4 3 2 1

CONTENTS

INTRODUCTION

Since the publication of *The Blessed Life* in 2001, I have been blessed to see the influence that the simple spiritual principle of generosity has had on millions of people throughout the world.

Generosity does, of course, mean giving. As with many things in life, however, the motivation behind any action is often as important—or more important—than the action itself. Unfortunately, the "give to get" message proclaimed from many pulpits and media over the last few decades suggests that the primary motivation for Christians to be generous givers is to get even more back in return.

On the contrary, I advocate "give to live" and "give to love" heart motivations for God's people. We should be generous because God was so generous to us. Our gracious God has offered us the most extravagant gifts imaginable—the gifts of salvation and eternal life with Him. As God's children and bearers of His image, believers should exhibit *His* kind of generosity. He is by nature a giver, and therefore, we should be givers, too.

When I wrote *The Blessed Life*, I assumed the reader would already accept the underlying assumption that *we have to live within our means*. It is a simple concept that *you can't give more than you have*. I did not address that issue in my book, but feedback since then has made me realize that there is still an unmet need in this area.

Beyond Blessed, then, is really a prequel to *The Blessed Life*—it is the first of the two legs on which a life of true blessing walks. Generosity is vitally important to experience the fullness of God's blessings, but understanding how to wisely manage one's financial resources comes first. The term for this management ability is *stewardship*. That is the focus of *Beyond Blessed*.

The apostle Paul was a great teacher and a mentor to Timothy. There was a great deal for student Timothy to learn. Paul's guidance to Timothy for that process was, "Study to shew thyself approved unto God" (2 Timothy 2:15 KJV). The purpose of this study guide is to provide a framework for you to fulfill that same instruction. Stewardship can be learned, and to learn, we need to study.

This study guide will lead you through each chapter of the book, expanding and presenting related material on some concepts, and challenging your thinking with questions and exercises. It will tie together the Bible's examples of stewards—good and bad—with real-life modern-day stories and people. It will help you apply scriptural instruction and principles, along with current information and literature, to the vital issues involved in wise stewardship.

You can use this study guide for individual study or as a guide for discussion and teaching within your family or in small groups.

Any material is easier to share if you have studied it yourself first. This is especially true of a topic that requires the kind of self-evaluation and soul-searching that stewardship does. To be honest, some of what you learn about yourself or your circumstances might seem quite painful. I would be surprised if that weren't the case for most readers.

Like the preacher in Ecclesiastes 5:10, I have tried to "find acceptable words . . . words of truth" to teach you.

Words are important; God *spoke* the Creation into being. Proverbs 18:21 says, "Death and life are in the power of the tongue." But while the Bible is the Word of God, the Bible is about more than words. The Bible comes alive through a Holy Spirit that works through emotions, sights, sounds, symbols, and experiences. Remember, the Holy Spirit is a friend—not just a force.

As you study *Beyond Blessed*, remember this basic, simple truth that we often miss:

> We are not physical beings living in a spiritual world. We
> are spiritual beings living in a temporary physical world!

God's infinite spiritual world is the context for every decision that believers make. Everything we say and do is important because it enables God's will to be done "on earth as it is in heaven" (Matthew 6:10), and because we are engaged in a spiritual battle with forces that know no boundaries except those that God places on them. And that battle is for believers' hearts.

God will bless, help, and reward your heartfelt efforts to be a better steward. I pray that the Spirit provides the insight, emotions, images, and experiences that will help take you to a place "beyond blessed."

CHAPTER ONE

MAXIMUM IMPACT, MINIMUM STRESS

I was raised in a household with wise and frugal parents. My father was and is a generous man who gave freely to the kingdom and those in need. He made loans to people without collateral and often without any real expectation of repayment. My father also managed his assets wisely so that he had the means to exercise that generosity. This model of frugal stewardship carried over into my marriage.

You may have grown up in a wealthy household or in poverty. However, stewardship is not dependent upon the level of your assets, but on spiritual attitude.

Were your parents generous? Did they manage their resources well, or did they tend to be extravagant and extend themselves financially?

_____

_____

_____

_____

Did your parents emphasize achieving success in a worldly manner at the expense of others, or did they encourage frugality and generosity in their children?

_____

_____

_____

_____

What other examples of generosity and stewardship have made an impression on you, either positive or negative? This could include influencers such as friends, family members, or others in your community or in public life.

_____

_____

_____

Considering the answers to the above questions, how has your thinking or your behavior relative to money and success changed as you matured in age? Which people or events had the greatest influence on your thinking or behavior?

_____

_____

_____

Imagine a life without financial stress. You (and your spouse, if you are married) are able to meet your own needs and routinely give to others with no requirement to be paid back. You seek out opportunities to bless people. At the same time, you are confident that you will be secure in your finances for the rest of your life.

When you imagined this life without financial stress, what were a couple of the most pleasant or satisfying experiences you imagined? Why were they so pleasant or satisfying?

_____

_____

_____

Assume that you have just won the lottery—not just a large scratch-off, but a massive, nine-figure prize that provides far more than enough for you to live comfortably. What do you think would be your initial reaction upon learning you won the prize? What would be the very first thing you would do with that money?

If you won the lottery, how do you think your close relatives and friends would react? What would they expect from you?

Assume that a close relative or your best friend won the same massive lottery prize. How do you think you would react to their good fortune? What would you expect from them?

The first important step toward stewardship is to settle the ownership issue. The first question to answer in that step is: *To whom do I belong?*

> Or do you not know that your body is the temple of the Holy Spirit who is in you, whom you have from God, and you are not your own? For you were bought at a price; therefore glorify God in your body and in your spirit, which are God's. (1 Corinthians 6:19–20)

> Whoever seeks to save his life will lose it, and whoever loses his life will preserve it. (Luke 17:33)

Therefore My Father loves Me, because I lay down My life that I may take it again. (John 10:17)

Then great multitudes came to Him, having with them the lame, blind, mute, maimed, and many others; and they laid them down at Jesus' feet, and He healed them. (Matthew 15:30)

According to these Scriptures, to whom do we belong? If you are a believer, what are some of the things that you have "laid down" in surrendering to Jesus? How did that make you feel?

_____

_____

_____

_____

Human kings sit on physical thrones, and the king's subjects show loyalty or obeisance to him by bringing a gift and laying it down in front of him. Notice that in the passage from Matthew, the "things" that the multitudes brought to Jesus and laid down at His feet were *people*.

The second fundamental question to answer is: *Who owns my stuff?*

The earth is the LORD's, and everything in it.
The world and all its people belong to him. (Psalm 24:1 NLT)

Here we see that the Scripture says explicitly that *people* belong to the Lord.

Do you have trouble releasing your attachment to or relinquishing ownership of things to God? If so, how does that specifically manifest in your thoughts and actions?

_____

_____

_____

Your daydream exercise earlier exhibited a life free from the pressure of money or fear of the unexpected. However, the 2014 Harris Poll showed that the majority of people feel stressed about money, and more than one in five experience extreme stress about money.

What level of stress do you experience about money or the lack of it? If your stress level is high, in what ways do you think it might affect you?

The fundamental issue behind this stress and poor stewardship is the failure to recognize that all things belong to God. That means that we do not put God first in our lives. And when something *other* than God occupies that place, that thing is an idol, and the result is idolatry. This is not just an Old Testament concept like the construction of the golden calf by the Israelites at Mount Sinai. The apostle John said, "Little children, keep yourselves from idols. Amen" (1 John 5:21 KJV).

Is money itself an idol in your life? Are there other things in your life that you recognize to be idols? How do you react to the simple idea that basic things can be idols, just like the golden calf of the Israelites?

I sought the LORD, and He heard me,
And delivered me from all my fears. (Psalm 34:4)

For God has not given us a spirit of fear, but of power and of love and
of a sound mind. (2 Timothy 1:7)

Give, and you will receive. Your gift will return to you in full—
pressed down, shaken together to make room for more, running
over, and poured into your lap. The amount you give will determine the amount you get back. (Luke 6:38 NLT)

The threshing floors will again be piled high with grain,
And the presses will overflow with new wine and olive oil. (Joel 2:24 NLT)

Two things contribute to our resistance to God's instructions about
tithes, generosity, and submission to Him in spending decisions: fear and a
scarcity mentality.

Which of these two things applies to you? Take some time to think about
this and explain.

_____

_____

_____

_____

Read 1 Corinthians 6:19–20 again and consider God's ownership of all
things.

Explain in your own words what I mean by the stewardship paradigm.

_____

_____

_____

_____

In your current residence, are you a tenant or do you own your own
home? In your relationship with the things of this world, are you ready to
make the paradigm shift from ownership to stewardship? Explain.

Key Quotes:

"Picture yourself being free to follow to the fullest the adventure God wants to live alongside you."

"Wherever you stand right now, however ill-equipped you may feel,...you can take the first crucial steps today—then follow through all the way to a life 'beyond blessed.'"

"There isn't anything in your life that didn't come from God's creation."

"When you return to God what's already His, you lock down a conviction, deep inside you, that God is...100 percent real and active in your life....You've now put your money where your heart is."

CHAPTER TWO

MORE THAN A BUDGET

If you have ever rented or stayed by yourself in someone else's home, such as on a vacation, you have probably experienced the feeling of being a stranger there. Unless you had been there several times before, you would have had to find out where things were and might even have been hypersensitive to certain items or areas.

You made yourself at home, but the owner's pictures on the walls, the personal items in each room, and even the contents of the pantry might have reminded you that this was not *your* home.

You were a guest in that home. You slept in the beds, sat on the couch, cooked in the kitchen, and watched the TV. Most likely, you even shared Wi-Fi for internet access. You were careful not to break anything or leave a mess behind (especially if there was a damage deposit the owner would return if you left it spotless).

When you rent a home through an agency like Airbnb or VRBO, you, as a renter, are rated according to how you act while you are there and the condition in which you leave the property. You are expected to treat it as well as, or better than, the owner would. If you do not, your renter's privileges might be restricted and your options limited. If you get enough bad ratings, you might have your privileges revoked entirely.

Have you ever stayed in someone else's home, either as a guest or through an agency? If so, how did you think and feel about the property during your stay? Were you especially careful of your surroundings? Did you feel a sense of responsibility?

_____

_____

_____

_____

If you haven't stayed in a home like that, can you still imagine the thoughts and feelings of being a stranger in another person's home? Explain.

_____

_____

_____

_____

"Few people understand that abundance is a far tougher test of character than poverty." Do you agree with this statement? Explain.

_____

_____

_____

_____

Jesus' parable in the twenty-fifth chapter of Matthew is where we will find a vivid example of faithful stewardship in the operation of God's economy.

> For the kingdom of heaven is like a man traveling to a far country, who called his own servants and delivered his goods to them. And to one he gave five talents, to another two, and to another one, to each according to his own ability; and immediately he went on a journey. Then he who had received the five talents went and traded with them, and made another five talents. And

likewise he who had received two gained two more also. But he who had received one went and dug in the ground, and hid his lord's money. After a long time the lord of those servants came and settled accounts with them.

So he who had received five talents came and brought five other talents, saying, "LORD, you delivered to me five talents; look, I have gained five more talents besides them." His lord said to him, "Well done, good and faithful servant; you were faithful over a few things, I will make you ruler over many things. Enter into the joy of your lord." He also who had received two talents came and said, "LORD, you delivered to me two talents; look, I have gained two more talents besides them." His lord said to him, "Well done, good and faithful servant; you have been faithful over a few things, I will make you ruler over many things. Enter into the joy of your lord."

Then he who had received the one talent came and said, "LORD, I knew you to be a hard man, reaping where you have not sown, and gathering where you have not scattered seed. And I was afraid, and went and hid your talent in the ground. Look, there you have what is yours."

But his lord answered and said to him, "You wicked and lazy servant, you knew that I reap where I have not sown, and gather where I have not scattered seed. So you ought to have deposited my money with the bankers, and at my coming I would have received back my own with interest. So take the talent from him, and give it to him who has ten talents.

"For to everyone who has, more will be given, and he will have abundance; but from him who does not have, even what he has will be taken away. And cast the unprofitable servant into the outer darkness. There will be weeping and gnashing of teeth." (Matthew 25:15–30)

Why did the master entrust his wealth (talents) to the three servants in the first place? How much was a talent worth?

_____

_____

_____

_____

We don't see any communication between the servants and master when the master leaves. How do you think each servant felt about the goods they received at the time? Might they have been nervous? Excited? Worried? How do you think you would have felt in the same situation?

_____

_____

_____

_____

The master gave "to each according to his ability." At some point we are all in the same position the master was in. When you had the opportunity to delegate responsibility, financial or otherwise, to people in different amounts based on their ability—perhaps to children, friends, or coworkers—how did you judge what level of responsibility to entrust them with? What did you learn about those people based on those experiences?

_____

_____

_____

_____

People often think the quality of stewardship is based primarily on budgeting and debt levels. Is that what this parable is demonstrating? What is the real and *important* increase that God is seeking when we steward our time, gifts, and relationships? Explain.

_____

_____

_____

_____

_____

God also entrusts us with people. You have been or will be entrusted to parents or adult guardians, teachers, coaches, or other mentors as their stewardship responsibility. Some will be excellent stewards of *you*, and others may not be.

I related a story of an evangelist who stewarded me poorly. How would you rate some of the people who have stewarded you? Were there some that were particularly good as stewards? How about others that may have been unwise stewards like the example I gave? Explain.

_____

_____

_____

_____

How do you break the cycle of bad stewardship? Do you have some examples from your own experience where you had to reverse that cycle?

_____

_____

_____

_____

But why do you judge your brother? Or why do you show contempt for your brother? For we shall all stand before the judgment seat of Christ. For it is written:

"As I live, says the LORD,
Every knee shall bow to Me,
And every tongue shall confess to God."

So then each of us shall give account of himself to God. (Romans 14:10–12)

The master in this parable came back to settle financial accounts (verse 19). Eventually however, all accounts—not just financial—will be settled.

Looking at your life right now, how would you honestly judge the quality of your stewardship overall? Would it be more like the "good and faithful servant" of Matthew 25:23, or the unprofitable servant in verses 28–30? Explain.

_____

_____

_____

_____

Jesus, in Mathew 6:20, encourages us to "lay up . . . treasures in heaven." This is likened to an ERA—Eternal Retirement Account. What do you think your ERA balance looks like now? Are you ready to become a better steward to build your ERA? How?

_____

_____

_____

_____

The one-talent steward told the master, "I knew you to be hard man." He was afraid of his master. For many believers, the root of their inability to handle money and material possessions like stewards rather than owners is a simple lack of trust in God.

How about you? Search your heart for your true feelings about how you view God. Read the story of the lost or "prodigal" son (Luke 15:11–32). Describe how you feel now and what changes you may need to make in your thinking and attitude.

_____

_____

_____

_____

_____

Key Quotes:

"It is the one who is faithful with a little who is ultimately entrusted with more. This is just as true of people as it is of money and possessions."

"Truly wise stewardship involves so much more than just following a budget."

"Being a wise steward of a great king actually means bringing increase to that ruler's kingdom, . . . It ultimately won't be about money. It will be about souls."

"Here is wonderful news. No matter what kind of steward you've been up to this point in life . . . you're not stuck in that category."

"A wrong view of God will invariably lead you to a wrong approach to the stewardship of the things He has entrusted to you."

CHAPTER THREE

YOUR PERSPECTIVE ON PROVISION

There are a number of famous roads you may be familiar with. Lombard Street in San Francisco contains eight hairpin turns in just one steep block. There is the famous "Strip," which is actually Las Vegas Boulevard. On one road in New Zealand, when you release your parking brake at the bottom, you roll uphill! Or so it seems, since the uphill perspective is an optical illusion. Many of us have come to a fork and taken "the road less traveled." And of course, most all of us have heard of the Beatles' Abbey Road in North London, which was also the title of their eleventh album.

The road of stewardship bears quite a resemblance to another, much more forbidding road: a forty-mile stretch of highway in Bolivia known as Old Yungas Road. It is a treacherous gravel road with no guardrails, high up in the Andes Mountains. There are sheer cliffs on either side of the road, often plunging hundreds, or even thousands, of feet. It is frequently muddy and slick due to tropical rains. On average, over two hundred people fall to their deaths each year. No wonder locals call it the Road of Death. The slightest driving mistake to either side can have fatal consequences.

What makes Old Yungas Road similar to Stewardship Road is that, in some places, there are sheer drop-offs on *both* sides. Fortunately, the drop-offs from Stewardship Road are ditches, not cliffs; a wrong turn from the Stewardship Road is not fatal. But they represent two mind-sets you can get stuck in—the poverty mind-set and the prosperity-materialism mind-set.

What is your first reaction when you think about Christians who are poor? Do you tend to assume that they are lazy and don't work hard or that they must have come upon some misfortune? Is their poverty directly related to their own actions and attitudes or is it a result of something that God causes or imposes on them?

_____

_____

_____

_____

Do you think there are advantages to being poor? If so, explain.

_____

_____

_____

_____

The formal word in Church history for the poverty mind-set is *asceticism*. What do you think of when you hear that word? What has been your impression of men and women like St. Francis of Assisi who have taken ascetic vows of poverty and lived solitary lives in monasteries?

_____

_____

_____

_____

Consider Jesus' teachings about the rich young ruler selling all his possessions (Mark 10:17–22) and it being easier for a camel to pass through the eye of a needle than for a rich man to get to heaven (Mark 10:25). How do these teachings relate to poverty?

_____

_____

_____

_____

_____

Read Matthew 5:3. Who was Jesus actually talking about in this passage? What does it mean that the poor in spirit will possess the kingdom of heaven?

_____

_____

_____

_____

What is the difference between asceticism and gnosticism? How are they related when considering the issue of God's provision?

_____

_____

_____

_____

Read 1 Timothy 6:17. What does it mean to enjoy things without loving them? Give some examples. Are there any things in your life that you can identify where you have dangerously moved from enjoying them to loving them?

_____

_____

_____

_____

A spirit of pride is often at the root of the poverty mind-set. Consider each of the five messages that are symptoms of the spirit of poverty. What are some examples from your own life where you are (or have been in the past) afflicted with each symptom? Or, write down something you may have noticed in someone you are very close to.

• The spirit of poverty tells us that stuff comes from the devil.

_____

_____

_____

- The spirit of poverty tells us to be ashamed of our stuff.

_____

_____

_____

- The spirit of poverty makes us think that we paid less than we really did.

_____

_____

_____

- The spirit of poverty makes us feel the need to justify all our purchases.

_____

_____

_____

- The spirit of poverty tries to make us feel guilty for God's blessings.

_____

_____

_____

Since asceticism is not a godly attitude and material possessions are not bad, does that mean you can just accumulate as much of any kind of stuff as you want? Or is simplicity still a virtue? Explain.

_____

_____

_____

_____

According to the text, with what attitude are we supposed to approach all the gifts God provides?

_____

_____

_____

_____

The second pitfall of rightly relating to money (the ditch on the *other* side of the road) is a materialistic mind-set that is often called the prosperity gospel: *You need to get everything you can out of life. After all, the one who dies with the most toys wins.* Materialism says that you have earned it and you deserve it. This is the mirror image of the poverty mind-set.

What do you think when you hear famous wealthy men like John D. Rockefeller and Andrew Carnegie talk about the problems associated with great wealth? How does this relate to the "deceitfulness of riches" in Mark 4:19?

_____

_____

_____

_____

Several falsehoods feed the idea that you would be happy and secure if you had more money: You need more. You deserve more. You're incomplete unless you get more. You'd be happier if you had more.

In 1 John 2:16 these lies are referred to as "the lust of the flesh, the lust of the eyes, and the pride of life." The spirit of materialism attaches our *self-worth* to our *net worth*. We are bombarded by the media with millions of messages that reinforce the wrong value that things will make us better and happier.

How often have you heard and believed these lies? How have you dealt with them in the past? Write down some specific examples and explain.

_____

_____

_____

_____

Read Matthew 6:24 in the King James Version. What does the word "Mammon" mean and how does it relate to the word used for "riches" in Mark 4:19?

_____

_____

_____

Read Revelation chapter 13. How does the character of "the beast" (the anti-Christ) and the way he will wield influence in the end-times relate to the spirit of Mammon? Why is this truth such a powerful warning to Christians about *who we must serve*? Consider this in the context of the enemy's appeal to us to turn into either of the two ditches: asceticism or the love of and dependence on money instead of God.

_____

_____

_____

Walking the Stewardship Road enables you to do well in every area of your life—spirit, soul, and body. God's blessings extend well beyond your pocketbook. He wants you to experience *prosperity*.

Prosperity is not measured in material things. It means "having the wind of God's Spirit in your sails as you move through life." God does not want us to be poor or, necessarily, to be rich.

Read the story of the rich young ruler in Mark 10:21. Why, *in Jesus' eyes*, did the young man walk away with his stuff?

_____

_____

_____

In your own words, what does it mean that we are called to live out our lives on a mission?

_____

_____

_____

_____

Based on your answer to the last question, write out a personal mission statement below. If you are married, include your spouse in this exercise. If you have children who are old enough, ask them to briefly answer this question as well.

_____

_____

_____

_____

Key Quotes:

"God doesn't mind us having things, but He never wants things to have us."

"We can be focused on God's agenda because we're so confident in His love, care, and faithfulness."

"The fact is that our God is a God of growth and increase."

"Whereas the spirit of poverty tells you that stuff comes from the devil, materialism convinces you that you earned it and deserve it."

"In a very real sense, Mammon is actually an anti-Christ spirit."

"Put as simply as I know how...stuff is stuff. God is not into stuff, God is into hearts."

CHAPTER FOUR

THE CFO OF "YOU, INC."

The Bible speaks a great deal about money, but not so much about what we would call a modern corporation. After all, the world of business was not as sophisticated in the agrarian society of Bible times.

Today's budding entrepreneurs would be more likely to audition for a spot on the immensely popular reality show *Shark Tank*. Now entering its tenth season and nearing two hundred episodes, this program features start-ups, early-stage inventors, and business people each making a pitch to five wealthy investors. Their goal is to get one or more of these "sharks" to invest a certain amount of money in their company in exchange for some amount of equity—a percentage ownership of the business.

Each participant on the show has a story of some kind. Most have started from small ideas and built up businesses with their own funds, and now they need money to grow. Some have little more than ideas or inventions. Regardless of the business, there is one thing that the sharks always consider important: Do they like and *trust* the entrepreneur that is making the pitch? Trust and believability have closed numerous financially marginal deals on the show and thwarted others that seemed to be financially sounder. Trust is a major factor when investing large sums of money or resources. Having a good CFO is crucial.

We started this chapter with an imaginary backstory to your own personal "company" parable.

To illustrate your position as the chief financial officer of a subsidiary of the universe's biggest enterprise, we imagined that you grew up as a runaway—alone, homeless, angry, and poor. As a teenager, you broke into the king's estate and vandalized its grounds and facilities. You slept in its barn and stole food from its storehouse. You did quite a bit of damage.

When you were finally caught and arrested, you were not treated as you expected you would be. You could have been enslaved, put into prison, or even executed. However, instead of pressing charges, the king paid for your defense, paid your fines, and forgave you.

Not only did he buy your freedom and give it back to you, he actually adopted you into his family. The king became your real father.

He also treated you equally with all his other children. He made you the co-heir of an enormous fortune beyond what you could comprehend.

Finally, when you grew up, he took you in as part of the family business. You were not just a laborer. He worked directly and personally with you and taught you everything you need to know about how to manage and govern the business of a wholly owned corporation—yourself.

He gave you independent decision-making power (free will) and watched how you served your customers and expanded the mission of the enterprise. He also rewarded you well when you were successful. The compensation package—salary, bonuses, and fringe benefits—was incredibly generous.

You are now the CFO of You, Inc., a subsidiary of God's universal holding company called The Kingdom. You want to grow your business for a lifetime. The question is: Are you up for the job? How will God—as He looks to further invest in your company—evaluate you?

> For if I do this thing willingly, I have a reward: but if against my will, a dispensation of the gospel is committed unto me. (1 Corinthians 9:17 KJV)

Whereof I am made a minister, according to the dispensation of God which is given to me for you, to fulfil the word of God. (Colossians 1:25 KJV)

In Ephesians 3:2, Paul writes that he had been given a "dispensation of the grace of God."

How is the Greek word dispensation (*oikonomia*) defined in these verses? (The New King James Version translates it as *stewardship* in 1 Corinthians.)

_____

_____

_____

_____

What does it mean to be entrusted with the dispensation of the gospel and the grace of God? What kind of responsibility does that imply for the believer?

_____

_____

_____

_____

Why should you be confident even though you don't have the skill set of a typical CFO for this position? Who is the Helper that will always be available to guide you and carry you along supernaturally?

_____

_____

_____

_____

What responsibilities did CEO God delegate to His first staff members in the Garden of Eden in Genesis 1:28?

_____

_____

_____

_____

All authority has been given to Me in heaven and on earth. Go therefore and make disciples of all the nations, baptizing them in the name of the Father and of the Son and of the Holy Spirit, teaching them to observe all things that I have commanded you; and lo, I am with you always, even to the end of the age. (Matthew 28:18–20)

In this well-known passage, Jesus delegates authority to His followers. He wants us to experience the joy and rewards of our labor with Him.

How does Jesus' great commission to His disciples (which was then delegated down to us) compare with the instructions God gave to Adam and Eve in the Garden? Explain.

_____

_____

_____

How does God feel about each one of His disciples as he or she carries out the building of their personal enterprise? Is He harsh and demanding, or is He caring, understanding, and encouraging? Explain.

_____

_____

_____

As with any position in any company, you have to start at the bottom and work your way up. God has given you control over a small branch of His kingdom, one in which you will wear many hats.

He who is faithful in what is least is faithful also in much; and he who is unjust in what is least is unjust also in much. (Luke 16:10)

In this passage, Jesus reminds us that we will all have to work our way up through the organization. We will be judged according to our performance.

How will we be judged? Going back to the parable of the talents, why did the unfaithful steward react the way he did? What was the reason he gave for doing nothing with his talent? What was the underlying emotion for his action? Explain.

_____

_____

_____

_____

This last issue is also important in the modern-day analysis of new businesses by the sharks. Some entrepreneurs are not able to handle the small things well, and/or failed to bring in outside expertise to help. Many times, the sharks opt not to invest based on their assessment that the company is a "product," not a "business." The sharks would be hesitant to commit more resources to such concepts.

How does God determine whether to make more or fewer resources available to His stewards? Can you give some examples, either from your own experience or the lives of others, where you could see God increase or decrease a believer's responsibility based on how well they managed what God had given them?

_____

_____

_____

_____

God is always redirecting resources to those who will partner with Him in sharing the gospel and building the kingdom. If we want to participate with God in growing our personal enterprise, we need to constantly evaluate the performance of the enterprise: We need to continually evaluate our hearts and the motivation behind our actions.

Based upon the parable of the talents, how does God feel about the unfaithful steward merely maintaining what the master had given him?

Should the master have been pleased that at least the talent had been preserved and returned to Him?

_____

_____

_____

_____

Consider the action of the unfaithful steward in light of the instructions of the Great Commission in Matthew 28:18–20. What would the kingdom look like today if the disciples, and those that they instructed to follow the same things Jesus commanded, had solely *maintained* their resources? In other words, how many believers would there be today if the disciples had been "one-talent" servants—if they had buried the gospel and never used it to take new ground?

_____

_____

_____

_____

For to everyone who has, more will be given, and he will have abundance; but from him who does not have, even what he has will be taken away. (Matthew 25:29)

God took the one talent from the unfaithful servant and gave it to the ten-talent servant. Is that fair? Why or why not? How was the master's initial distribution of the talents determined in the first place?

_____

_____

_____

_____

Based on the text, fill in the blanks: "Good stewards are entrusted with _____ and bad stewards are entrusted with _____."

To what groups of people is God particularly interested in showing generosity and compassion? Why does He choose those groups?

_____

_____

_____

_____

God is looking for servants He can bless. What is the immense sacrifice that God Himself wants to steward well and how does that carry over into all of our stewardship? (See Hebrews 10:10.)

_____

_____

_____

_____

He who is faithful in what is least is faithful also in much; and he who is unjust in what is least is unjust also in much. Therefore if you have not been faithful in the unrighteous mammon, who will commit to your trust the true riches? And if you have not been faithful in what is another man's, who will give you what is your own? (Luke 16:10–12)

Let me rephrase these verses that summarize stewardship:

"If God can't trust you with a little, He can't trust you with a lot." (v. 10)

"If I can't trust you with mere money (which will perish), I can't trust you with ministry (which is much more important because it is eternal). For heaven's sake, if I can't trust you with a dollar bill, I certainly can't trust you with a priceless soul." (v. 11)

"If you're not faithful with what someone else entrusts to you, I'm sorry, but I can't give you your own." (v. 12)

Good stewardship is important to God. How do you feel about developing the vital skills, habits, and values that comprise good stewardship? How do you think God feels about your efforts?

_____

_____

_____

According to the book, what three things do all good stewards do?

_____

_____

_____

The tricky thing about being a subsidiary in this kingdom is that it is largely invisible. It is a bit more difficult to work for an unseen Chairman of the Board who may not speak to you in an audible voice or enforce His accountability directly. But God is real even though He is unseen. And the day of accountability when He will reveal the results of how we steward His gifts is also quite real.

In light of this fact, read Hebrews 11:1. According to this verse, what is the primary currency of the Christian faith that we steward? In other words, what enables us to remember that we are stewarding the assets entrusted to us by an invisible, intangible Owner?

_____

_____

_____

_____

Key Quotes:

"God is looking for good stewards because He loves people."

"You don't steward God's blessings by stuffing them into a box and burying them—you steward them by letting them live and breathe with you and by diligently and intentionally nurturing them into growth."

"Paul viewed his life and calling in terms of stewarding a spiritual business enterprise. . . . Shouldn't we do so as well?"

"If we want to participate with God in growing our personal enterprise, we need to constantly evaluate the performance of the enterprise."

"Despite His invisibility, God is more real than any physical object you can see, touch, taste, hear, or smell. That day of accounting in which He reviews the results of our stewardship of His gifts is also quite real."

CHAPTER FIVE

FIRST THINGS FIRST

The story of Dave and Julie, in various forms, is one I have seen manifest itself frequently throughout my years of ministry. Many of you reading this book have been (or still are) in a similar situation at some time in your life.

The immediate issue was a job search for a way to provide more income and more time for Dave with his family. This couple was struggling with the challenge of raising children, putting them through college, and making ends meet, including paying off medical bills from their daughter's successful battle with cancer. They were doing this on one income from a job that made it difficult for Dave to find quality time with his family.

While this story results in a blessing related to tithing, the *first* step in Dave's breakthrough was not a decision about money itself. It required a personal breakthrough of faith.

If you know my personal story, I led quite a rebellious and immoral life in my late teenage years. I still often wonder how Debbie could have been attracted to me.

Dave, while driving to work and listening to my testimony about how God transformed my life as a college-age man—from one of immorality to trust in the Lord—was moved to examine his own salvation and decided that he was not sure that he was saved. Right there, in his car, he gave his life to Jesus. Notice that the effect on him was emotional and immediate.

That is what often happens when you have a close encounter with the King of the universe.

Think about a time where you were unsure of what direction to take about a major area of your life. What were (or are) the issues involved? How did you approach the situation? What decisions did you make? What was the result?

_____

_____

_____

_____

If you are dealing with a major decision now, how will the example of Dave and Julie affect your approach?

_____

_____

_____

_____

Are you comfortable with your personal, eternal relationship with God? Are you sure that you are saved? If not, will you deal with that issue *first* by accepting Jesus and dedicating your life to God?

_____

_____

_____

_____

Dave's encounter led him to learn and want more of God, and he and Julie dove into the teachings at Gateway Church, including attending the stewardship course. This is when the decision about finances came to the forefront. They realized that their old way of looking at finances and giving was not working. The alternative—giving away the first 10 percent of their income—didn't make sense to their natural minds. Nevertheless, they gave their first tithe. The rest, as they say, is history—and a powerful testimony. Dave immediately got a new and better job from an unsolicited source. Within a few years, their financial situation had turned around completely.

Have you experienced a major breakthrough in any area of your life that you recognized as God's provision? What was that breakthrough? How did you feel when it happened? Did you share that experience with others?

_____

_____

_____

_____

The principle of *first things first* is a common cliché. Many of us have read or heard of Stephen Covey's 1994 book of the same name. His work is well-known for its advice on establishing priorities. He addresses at length the concept of the "tyranny of the urgent," where the seemingly urgent issues in life draw us away from what is important. (The term "tyranny of the urgent" was first introduced in a 1967 booklet by Charles Hummel.)

The principle of *first things first* sounds simple, but in fact can be a difficult concept to implement. In an agricultural society where the cows *had* to be milked every morning and the crops would be destroyed if they were not harvested in time, some "firsts" were relatively obvious. Today's society moves at a pace that is unprecedented. We are constantly bombarded with texts, tweets, and emails that we assume are "urgent."

God, however, in His infinite wisdom, gave us a plan to establish our priorities.

Read Genesis 2:15–17. What is God saying to Adam and Eve about priorities?

_____

_____

_____

_____

Read Exodus 20:3. What is the *first* commandment God gave to Moses for the Israelites?

_____

_____

_____

_____

The commandment to put God first is as applicable to us today as it was to the Israelites in the Old Testament. It is, simply put, an admonition against idolatry. The apostle John closed his book of First John with these words:

Dear children, keep yourselves from idols. (5:21 NIV)

How can you know that you are putting God first and not worshipping a false god—an idol? Whatever provides your sense of identity is what you worship. Whatever provides a sense of security is what you worship. Whatever you seek out first—that's what you worship.

What things or people in your life provide you with a sense of identity? Of security? What things first come to mind that might be idols in your life? What will you do to make God a priority compared to those things?

_____

_____

_____

_____

Another way that God helps us set priorities is with the principle of *firstfruits*. The principle is established throughout Leviticus, Numbers, and Exodus as God asks the people to bring to the priests of the tabernacle the very first crops to have ripened.

Read Exodus 23.19 and 34.26. What is God asking the people to bring Him?

_____

_____

_____

_____

The complete answer to that question is the *first* of the firstfruits. This principle is carried forward to the first of other firstfruits as well.

> Consecrate to Me all the firstborn, whatever opens the womb among the children of Israel, both of man and beast; it is Mine. (Exodus 13:2)

Here, and fifteen other times in Scripture, God lays claim to the firstborn. And of course, God ultimately redeemed us back with His own innocent, spotless firstborn: Jesus was God's firstfruits offering.

Besides money, what are some other things to which you could apply the principle of firstfruits? How might you do that?

_____

_____

_____

_____

Finances seem to be the area in which Christians struggle the most with putting God first. We have already seen how the spirit of Mammon attached itself to money and wants to be worshipped. Many people look to money to provide their sense of identity and security.

In this fast-paced age of information overload and constant bombardment with messages from television and the internet, much of the focus is on financial matters. What to buy, how to invest, and where to contribute are portrayed as urgent and important issues. We can monitor the financial markets from our cell phones. (And we can tune in to watch new episodes or reruns of *Shark Tank* almost any day of the week.)

What other things in the media besides money compete for your attention? Write down some of the messages that you notice. Perhaps it is a home remodeling show or an investing program. What commercials do you remember?

_____

_____

_____

_____

The answer for what to give God as firstfruits is a simple one. The tithe. *Tithe* means one-tenth, and the biblical principle is to give a tenth of your increase. (See Proverbs 3:9–10.)

You can find a more extensive teaching about tithing in my book *The Blessed Life*.

What have you been taught in the past about tithing? How do you feel about tithing?

_____

_____

_____

_____

Why does God want you to tithe? In what is He really interested? Is the stewardship practice of faithfully tithing for and about God? Explain.

_____

_____

_____

_____

"The tithe is both a reminder and a test." Of what is the tithe a reminder and what does the principle of tithing test?

_____

_____

_____

_____

"The tithe is much more than a test. It's actually a spiritual gateway for God to enter your circumstances and place His blessing on the remaining 90 percent of your income."

In cooking terms, in order to make new sourdough bread, you save a small portion of the dough to use in the next loaf. This starter is what keeps the life of this kind of bread going.

In scriptural terms, the firstfruits offering redeems the remaining portion. The first portion carries the blessing. It keeps life going.

> For if the firstfruit is holy, the lump is also holy; and if the root is holy, so are the branches. (Romans 11:16)

Scripture is replete with examples of this principle.

Read Genesis 4:1–12, Joshua 6, and Matthew 6:33. How is the principle of first applied in each story and situation? To what *things* is the principle applied?

_____

_____

_____

_____

Read the story of Elijah and the widow in 1 Kings 17. How long did her flour last and her oil not run dry?

_____

_____

_____

_____

God provided miraculous provision for Elijah in the wilderness before He sent Elijah to the widow in Zarephath, where God said that a widow would provide for him. What was the real reason that God sent Elijah to the widow? Explain your answer.

_____

_____

_____

_____

What happened later in 1 Kings 17 that shows the tithe affects more than money? How do you think the widow felt about the second miracle compared to the first?

_____

_____

_____

_____

_____

Read Malachi 3:10–11. How do you feel about the prospect of the Lord opening up to you this kind of overflowing blessing? Are you ready to receive it?

_____

_____

_____

_____

_____

In chapter two I asked you to read the parable of the prodigal son in Luke 15. In verse 31, the father says to the older son who remained behind, "Son, you are always with me, and all that I have is yours."

Both of the sons were engaged in spiritual warfare. The younger son had, by this time, completed most of his battles. He was on his way back to acceptance and redemption—from absence to presence with his father.

The older son was grieved that the return of the younger son was celebrated. I believe that the older son, even though he stayed at home with his father, was not *with* his father. The older son was still fighting the most basic of battles.

We must always begin by basking in God's presence. There are many battles, but the first battle to prepare for is what I call the "everyday battle." It is the practice of spending quiet time with the Lord. You win this battle just by showing up! Here are four guidelines the Lord gave me some years ago for my quiet time. They might vary for you, but I hope they help.

1. Quiet your mind. Take a few minutes in silence to help remove distracting thoughts.
2. Focus your mind. For me, this means to sing. Invite the Lord into your thoughts with praise.
3. Pray your mind. Pray about the personal things that are on your mind.
4. Renew your mind with God's Word. Read something in the Bible.

Spend some quiet time with the Lord about how to set your priorities for stewardship. Write down what the Holy Spirit is saying to you.

_____

_____

_____

_____

Key Quotes:

"God went to so much trouble to help us prioritize things properly."

"If you want to live a life beyond blessed, God must be first. This isn't for His benefit. It's for yours."

"Whatever you seek out *first*—that's what you worship."

"Sixteen times in Scripture God lays claim to the firstborn....Jesus was God's firstfruits offering."

"God did not send Elijah to the widow to provide for Elijah—He sent Elijah to provide for the widow."

CHAPTER SIX

HUMBLY GRATEFUL, NOT GRUMBLY HATEFUL

It all depends on your perspective—and your expectations.

When Andy, a longtime member of Gateway Church, volunteered to travel to Luanda, Angola, with James Robison's LIFE Outreach International team, he was certainly aware that he was not going on a trip to the French Riviera. I doubt that he even brought along a bathing suit.

He probably also did not expect to be staying at the Ritz-Carlton, though some major cities in lesser-developed countries do have a Hilton or Hyatt of reasonable quality that is used by expatriates.

Nevertheless, he was shocked by what he saw upon his arrival in the city. Open sewers, abandoned cars, garbage-littered streets, and gaunt stray dogs, along with an indescribable stench, comprised his initial impression of the city—including the hotel where they were to spend their first night before traveling on to the rural area where they would be staying for the next week. The hotel cost what a Hyatt or Hilton would have cost, but the quality was not comparable.

What Andy saw in the rural towns compounded his shock even further. Horribly poor sanitation, lack of clean water, crumbling (if any) infrastructure, and inadequate medical facilities and services were the norm. The city looked like a war zone, and the countryside must have looked like a scene from a postapocalyptic movie.

Have you ever been to an extremely poor third-world country and witnessed the kind of poverty and conditions described in this chapter? If not, do you know someone personally who has traveled to or worked in a country with those kinds of conditions (perhaps in the Peace Corps or on a mission trip)? What were your thoughts and impressions based on either your personal observations or the accounts, descriptions, pictures, or videos of others?

_____

_____

_____

_____

Andy's trip would have affected him regardless of his circumstances. But the impact was particularly significant to him because of the perspective that Andy had at that time about material things in his environment.

Prior to the trip, Andy lived a relatively comfortable, if simple, suburban lifestyle with a happy family life, close friends, and little debt to worry about. Yet, as he saw more and more of the affluence around him, he became less content with his situation and wanted more of what others had: the larger house, the nicer neighborhood, the fancy sports car. From his perspective—seeing so much of what the nearby upper class had—his expectations were growing.

That was until he saw the face of a young, barefoot boy playing with a stick and a bicycle wheel on a filthy dirt street in Luanda: the face that flashed an expression of pure delight. Joy. Freedom.

What was Andy's reaction to seeing the boy in Luanda? What emotions did it evoke and what response did it produce in him? What supernatural force do you believe was behind that reaction and response?

_____

_____

_____

_____

Read James 4:1–3. Where does all this envy, anger, and discontent come from?

_____

_____

_____

Yes, materialism and ingratitude for our blessings cause us to resent the blessings of others and cut us off from the additional blessings God wants for our lives. A grateful heart is a key to successful stewardship.

> In everything give thanks; for this is the will of God in Christ Jesus for you. (1 Thessalonians 5:18)

> Enter into his gates with thanksgiving, and into his courts with praise: be thankful unto him, and bless his name. (Psalm 100:4 KJV)

As we noted in chapter four, God does not want us to engage in a poverty mind-set. However, He also does not expect us to covet what others have and lose sight of all that He has done for us.

Take an honest inventory here. What things or circumstances in your life are you truly grateful for? Count your blessings. What can you identify that you may have a desire for that is either not scriptural or is excessive? Are you attracted to a "prosperity" gospel?

_____

_____

_____

_____

Consider the impact of Andy's story and what we have discussed in this chapter so far. Has your thinking and attitude been influenced in any way? Explain.

_____

_____

_____

_____

_____

Because, although they knew God, they did not glorify Him as God, nor were thankful, but became futile in their thoughts, and their foolish hearts were darkened. Professing to be wise, they became fools, and changed the glory of the incorruptible God into an image made like corruptible man—and birds and four-footed animals and creeping things.

Therefore God also gave them up to uncleanness, in the lusts of their hearts, to dishonor their bodies among themselves, who exchanged the truth of God for the lie, and worshiped and served the creature rather than the Creator, who is blessed forever. (Romans 1:21–25)

Unthankfulness can open the door to many bad things in your life. What are some of those things described in this passage of Paul's letter to the Romans?

_____

_____

_____

_____

_____

Read 2 Timothy 3:1–5. In this Scripture, what negative character qualities does Paul warn Timothy to look out for in the last days? What does Paul tell Timothy to do to "such people"?

_____

_____

_____

_____

Early in our marriage, I had rationalized the need to purchase a car with a monthly payment larger than our house payment. It took some time for me to finally listen to and accept God's leading to sell that car and replace it. God was clearly urging me to get our finances in order.

After we sold the car and paid off the note, we had exactly $750 in savings left over. We were able to use it to pay exactly that price for an old station wagon. This is the car I mentioned in _The Blessed Life_, and we felt such peace and joy in owning it. We loved it partly because our title was free and clear but also because we had obeyed God in buying it.

That purchase was also the beginning of a broader stewardship effort for Debbie and me. We got serious about our finances, and God got serious about supplying our needs. And He often did so in a supernatural manner.

What happens in the lives of believers, as evidenced in the experience Debbie and I had, when a believer pursues good stewardship?

_____

_____

_____

_____

Philippians 4:19 says, "And my God shall supply all your need according to His riches in glory by Christ Jesus." Discuss this verse in the context of this chapter.

_____

_____

_____

_____

The simple message of this chapter is to be grateful at all times—not just about money. Be grateful about everything. What are some of the things listed at the end of this chapter that we should be grateful for? Are there any you would add to the list?

_____

_____

_____

_____

What is the Holy Spirit saying to you about how to put finances in perspective and adjust your expectations?

_____

_____

_____

_____

Andy's perspective and expectations changed after his mission trip. He took away something very special when he left Angola after seeing that little boy.

As the father said to the elder son in Luke 15:31 and Jesus told His disciples in Matthew 28:20, *He is always with us.*

We know that God is everywhere—that is His omnipresence. When you are saved, His Holy Spirit comes and dwells in you—that is His inner presence. But there is more—His manifest presence—where God makes His presence known.

God walked with Adam and Eve in the garden (see Genesis 3:8). He told Moses and the Israelites his presence would go with them (see Exodus 33:14–15). Jonah tried to flee from God's presence (see Jonah 1:1–3).

King Saul was afraid of David because God was with him (see 1 Samuel 18:12). It is God's manifest presence that David took with him when he went out from worship into battle.

It is this form of His presence that we also enter into with worship and obedience, and we then take that presence out with us into our lives as we serve Him. When we do that, we will not only *be* in God's presence, we will *live* in His presence!

What can you do to experience more of His manifest presence?

_____

_____

_____

_____

Key Quotes:

"Then he caught a glimpse of the boy's face. It held an expression of pure delight. Joy. Freedom."

"I think a root cause of our current climate of anger is unthankfulness—along with its constant companions: envy, resentment, and discontent."

"My point is that a heart for faithful stewardship begins by being genuinely thankful for the lifestyle and standard of living you have *now*."

"The root of the problem in these situations isn't God's level of provision. It's our mismanagement of what He has provided."

"When we begin to set our finances in order, God supernaturally blesses us."

CHAPTER SEVEN

HAPPY HEART, HAPPY HOME

An attitude of gratitude is a vital component of living the blessed life and going beyond blessed. It is a necessary factor in a happy heart.

As we saw in the last chapter, our attitude and how we react to our circumstances—financial or otherwise—depend upon our perspective and personal expectations.

Andy saw the poverty in Angola firsthand. But if you are more of a numbers person, some statistics might help.

Perspective

Gross Domestic Product (GDP) is the total wealth production of a country annually.

The GDP of Angola in 2017 was approximately 190.3 billion US dollars. That amounted to a per capita GDP of $6,800. The per capita GDP of Angola is 161st out of 229 countries.[1]

The GDP of the United States in 2017 was approximately 19.4 trillion US dollars. That amounted to a per capita GDP of $59,500. That is 8.75 times as much per person as Angola. The total US GDP represents over 30 percent of the world's economy.[2] (Even then, there are 18 countries in the world with a *higher per capita GDP* than the US. I will leave it to you to look them up.)

Again, GDP is what we *produce* annually. That includes what we save, invest, and *spend*. So what about spending?

On an annualized basis, consumer spending in the United States was about 12.8 trillion in the second quarter of 2018.[3] Over 12.8 trillion US dollars—$40,000 per person, or about 65% of what was produced—was spent by consumers. The rest was saved, invested, or spent by the government.

Those numbers should help you gain some additional perspective with which to evaluate your finances. Perhaps even more important for our purposes, however, is considering the *expectations* we have.

Expectations

Here are some recent income and spending statistics from the Bureau of Economic Analysis. These are for the year 2018. As you read these numbers, remember that they are the amounts of ***increase***!

In July...Disposable personal income (DPI) increased $52.5 billion (0.3 percent) and personal consumption expenditures (PCE) increased $49.3 billion (0.4 percent).[4]

The percentage increases look small. However, the .4 percent increase in *spending* was 33.3 percent **greater** than the .3 percent increase in *income*!

What does the business world think about the US economy at this same time? The answer to that question is in the bold type from this *Wall Street Journal* article:

Americans have more money in their pockets, thanks to robust job growth, rising pay and a tax cut that took effect early this year. Household income—including what Americans earned from salaries and investments—rose 0.3% in July.

Also, the booming stock market and rising home values are raising Americans' wealth, **which tends to encourage them to spend more and save less.**

The fact that spending rose faster than income shows how confident Americans are in the economy these days. After accounting for inflation, consumer spending rose 2.8% in July, compared with the same month a year ago—an annual gain last exceeded in March 2017.

"It's encouraging to see that the American consumer continues to spend confidently and on a steady basis, with the streak in real spending gains extending to five months as of July," said Admir Kolaj, an economist at TD Economics, in a note to clients."[5] (emphasis added)

Increased income is good. Increased spending seems to be even better.

What is your reaction to these statistics about wealth and spending? What would you say to an "average" Angolan if he or she asked you about your finances?

_____

_____

_____

_____

How would you describe the difference between your economic perspective and expectations and those of the average Angolan?

_____

_____

_____

_____

If you look at the average growth in the US economy over the last sixty years, the trend in GDP has been steadily up except during the 2008–2009 recession. Should this constant growth of the economy encourage you to expect future growth? Considering God's economy, should we share the Wall Street Journal's optimistic assessment during this good time? Explain.

_____

_____

_____

_____

Consider again your answer to the previous question in light of two other statistics: The US national debt now stands at about $15 trillion; about 78 percent of GDP. The recent US tax cuts are projected to increase the national debt by $2.3 trillion over the next ten years.[6] Does knowing these numbers affect your thinking? If so, how?

_____

_____

_____

_____

The financial plight of Jack and Karen is all too common. They had a debt load of over $400,000. As I said, it is a textbook case for why I wrote this book. By the way, remember that I said student loan debt was a major portion of their problem? For perspective, consider one final statistic: The total outstanding student loan debt in the United States right now is about $1.5 trillion. Compare that to the GDP of Angola!

Financial mismanagement causes and contributes to many marital problems.

All relationships take time and effort. Learning to live together with an imperfect spouse (and we all are) takes time and effort in the best of marriages.

How do financial problems affect communication in a marriage? If you are married, what are some examples from your marriage? If you are not married, how did financial problems affect your parents and the rest of your family (even if there was just a single parent)? Can you recall specific communications about money that were stressful?

_____

_____

_____

_____

What other problems can mismanagement of finances cause besides relational problems? Give some personal examples from your experience.

_____

_____

_____

_____

The second commandment in my sermon series titled The Ten Financial Commandments was "Thou Shalt Not Try to Acquire Happiness Through Material Things." Like the second commandment God delivered through Moses, the issue is idolatry. We talked some about idolatry in chapters one and five.

The spirit of Mammon wants you to believe that more money or more stuff will make you happy. We need something better...something different...something more. You can always find something more or better than you have.

This desire takes many forms. We don't necessarily just name and daydream about a particular desire. The desire for a luxury item or a new home leads us to subscribe to magazines or blogs that reflect those desires. You may have pictures of that item or house on your refrigerator or on your desk at work to remind you of those desires.

Mammon uses many means to lead us in this direction.

You are constantly being motivated by outside influences to get more. We are, after all, incentive-driven people. If you work in sales, you have likely been offered all kinds of incentives to perform: bonuses, trips, cars, or selections from a catalog. Not that these things are wrong on their own— they just illustrate the mind-set that easily engulfs us.

There is the Publishers Clearing House sweepstakes and the Powerball lottery. (Remember what we learned about the troubles that sudden wealth can bring.) But on the other hand, you are encouraged to open a bank account in exchange for a toaster (Okay, that's in the old days) or a gift card. Even credit cards compete for your business on the basis of points that you can redeem for travel, goods, or simply cash back.

The internet makes it amazingly simple to indulge our fantasies. A generation ago, you'd have to read a magazine or request a brochure in the mail. You'd have to go to the bank to open an account. All you have to do today is get online, push a few keys, and you can find and buy (if you can afford it) anything your heart desires.

In order to break the cycle that King Solomon talks about in Proverbs 27:20, you must learn to recognize these attacks and learn the principle of delayed gratification. Avoid impulse purchases.

Have you ever been incentivized at your work, whether as a salesperson or just for general performance? How was that done? How did you respond to those incentives?

_____

_____

_____

_____

How much do financial incentives drive you? Are there specific things that particularly motivate you? Explain.

_____

_____

———————————————————————————

———————————————————————————

Take some time to think about specific purchases and the pattern of your spending and that of your family. Are you strongly subject to impulse buying? What can you do to avoid this habit?

———————————————————————————

———————————————————————————

———————————————————————————

———————————————————————————

Understand that we are all subject to these temptations and the attacks of the enemy. We must embrace in our hearts that *things* do not have the power to make us happy. And there is the heart of the matter. The issue is our *hearts*. God wants us to understand that what He offers us—things such as salvation, life, hope, and peace—are the things that have true value and that we should treasure above all else. That is true happiness.

> Finally, brethren, whatever things are true, whatever things are noble, whatever things are just, whatever things are pure, whatever things are lovely, whatever things are of good report, if there is any virtue and if there is anything praiseworthy—meditate on these things. (Philippians 4:8)

When we learn this truth, then we must also teach it to our children. Reject the lie that things provide happiness and constantly reinforce that message to your children. Allow the Spirit of God to work in your hearts so that you can understand and also teach the place and role of money.

Consider and pray about your own experience with the spirit of Mammon. Define in your own words the proper role of money. What is the next step you will take to deal with this issue?

———————————————————————————

———————————————————————————

_____

_____

If you are a parent, what have you taught your children about the role of money and things? What have you modeled for them in this area? What will you do differently going forward?

_____

_____

_____

There are many good resources available to help you become better stewards, and we will delve into some of those later. Jack and Karen began with a book by Dave Ramsey and did everything possible to eliminate their debt. Because of their good stewardship, God blessed them with greater income that they used to further attack their debt. In a little over two years, they were debt-free, but during that time they were also enjoying greater peace and harmony in their relationship.

I know that there have been quite a few statistics quoted in this section. However, they will provide a context for the topic in our next chapter, and I hope they will also provide perspective for you as we approach more practical, down-to-earth issues later.

Key Quotes:

"In my experience, mismanagement of finances causes more marital problems than any other cause."

"The spirit of Mammon's most effective and seductive lie is that more money or stuff will make you happy."

"My point is it's not the presence or absence of material possessions or wealth that determines happiness. But thinking that they do is a form of idolatry. And idolatry always leads to catastrophe."

"You will never get your finances in order until you break the hold of the spirit of Mammon."

"The ability to delay gratification...is one of the rarest and most powerful skills in our culture."

"The way you view and handle money...will be imparted to your children....Never teach your family—through words or actions—that having and spending money is the answer to problems. It's not."

CHAPTER EIGHT

THERE IS ENOUGH

In chapter seven we talked about the great lie the spirit of Mammon teaches: that possessing things can make us happy. Mammon has spawned a variety of schemes and villains throughout the twentieth century.

John Dillinger. Al Capone. Bonnie and Clyde. These are well-known villains who used traditional, violent criminal means to steal things. They were notoriously greedy and willing to kill anyone who got in their way.

Some villains are less well known. Though many people are familiar with the term "Ponzi scheme," not everyone knows that the name is derived from a notorious con man who made his fortune in the early 1920s. Charles Ponzi took investments from people and promised them a 50 to 100 percent return on their investment in just a few months. Of course, his plan was to take the money from new investors to pay returns to the early investors. Eventually, the plan fell apart, and investors lost tens of millions of dollars (in today's dollars).

The scheme has been duplicated many times over the years, but none quite like that of investment banker Bernie Madoff, who, by the time he was arrested in December 2008, had bilked investors out of nearly $65 billion! How long the scheme actually lasted is not known—authorities think it could have started as early as the 1970s.

You may be familiar with the story of Jordan Belfort: *The Wolf of Wall*

Street. His methods were not a Ponzi scheme, but Belfort's memoir of his and his colleagues' insatiable lust for money and power might well personify "the lust of the flesh and lust of the eyes" of 1 John 2:16.

Even corporations can get into the act. In 2001, Enron Corporation declared bankruptcy after years in which the company's executives "cooked the books" with fraudulent transactions, inflated revenues, and Ponzi-like investments. Several of their executives went to prison. The level of fraud? At the time of the bankruptcy, the company claimed over $63 billion in assets! And if you wonder how a public company of that size could get away with it for so long, you need to know that their auditor—Big Five public accounting firm Arthur Andersen—was indicted for obstruction of justice and found guilty of conspiring and destroying documents. They didn't assist in the theft, but they looked the other way. They also ceased to exist as a company as a result of the fraud.

Are you familiar with the names and events above? What is your visceral reaction to their crimes?

_____

_____

_____

_____

As despicable as these criminals were, millions of people are running a Ponzi scheme on themselves. They have conned themselves into believing that future earnings will inevitably be available to pay current expenditures. Like with the operations of Mr. Ponzi and Mr. Madoff, this path can only end in heartache and tears, with you being a prisoner.

How do we get to this place? As I said in the previous chapter, we like to think that we are logical, rational people. But our emotions and desires set us up to rationalize Mammon's lie that these things will make us happy.

Of course, as you saw in the *Wall Street Journal* article quoted in the previous chapter, there is plenty of logical, rational, external support for Mammon's argument as well.

The vast majority of impulse purchases appear to be explained—rationalized—by the fact that the item was on sale. However, if you buy enough things on sale, you could still go bankrupt.

According to the text, what physical manifestation (brain chemistry) takes place when you buy something that you crave?

_____

_____

_____

_____

The story of Pam and Eric shows just how real the "shopaholic" addiction is and what a toll it can take on a couple and their marriage.

Do you know someone (including yourself) who exhibits uncontrolled tendencies to buy things? What does that look like?

_____

_____

_____

_____

Spending money you don't have is a form of stealing—and God is against stealing: "You shall not steal" (Ex. 20:15). When you steal from yourself, it is still theft. And theft is the most instant form of instant gratification.

Have you ever stolen anything? What were the circumstances? What were the repercussions?

_____

_____

_____

_____

Have you ever had to deal with theft by anyone else? This could be theft by a friend or family member, including a child. What were the circumstances? How did you handle the situation?

_____

_____

———————————————

———————————————

———————————————

By now you will be aware that theft can mean taking things other than money or material possessions—perhaps wasting time or exhausting energy.

Answer these previous two questions again, considering any other form of theft (besides money or goods) that you may be able to identify.

———————————————

———————————————

———————————————

———————————————

Breaking this vicious cycle of spending and debt requires that you learn to wait.

For many of you this won't be easy. This will come to you as a trial. We all face trials and tribulations, but we often define these situations in terms of a struggle with something like disease, death, or severe hardship. But overspending is an addiction as debilitating as many drugs, often with similar consequences.

One term for learning to wait is patience. It is a fruit of the Spirit. And in case you think that patience just means casually waiting for something, read Galatians 5:22–23 in different versions. While the *English Standard Version* translates the word as *patience*, the *King James Version* and *New King James Version* use the term *longsuffering*. *The New International Version* translates it as *forbearance*.

The practice of buy-now-and-pay-later is financial suicide–both individually and as a culture. The high rate of personal indebtedness and high rate of depression in the United States are related.

We see from the story of Abraham how his initial lack of patience birthed Ishmael and a host of problems, but when he went back to waiting on God, his expectation was fulfilled as God had promised.

Even when there was no reason for hope, Abraham kept hoping—believing that he would become the father of many nations. For God had said to him, "That's how many descendants you will have!" (Romans 4:18 NLT)

Read Romans 5:3–5 and James 1:1–12 and you will realize that the path always leads from trial or tribulation to patience (perseverance) and eventually to hope. We are designed to run on hope, and borrowing is a hope killer.

Do you consider yourself a hopeful person? What do you think of when you think of *your* hope for the future? Explain.

_____

_____

_____

_____

Debt has been around as long as there have been people. God gave His people laws against *usury*, and archaeological records from as far back as 3500 BC record the use of debt and interest.

However, the levels of debt and means of incurring debt have skyrocketed in the last century. Mortgages as we know them weren't widely available until the 1930s, and loans were for shorter terms and could only be for 50 percent of the home's market value.

In 1934, American Airlines began offering an air travel card to enable the general public to afford air travel by paying in installments. It was the first such installment card. Diners Club and American Express offered "charge cards" in the 1950s, but the first true "credit card" was created in 1960. That was the BankAmericard, now known as Visa. Today, credit card offers arrive at most of our homes almost every day, sometimes addressed to our children who are minors and don't have a job. I've even seen them addressed to pets.

How did your parents or grandparents (or friends that you know) who grew up in the first half of the twentieth century feel about debt?

_____

_____

_____

_____

As we saw with the example of Jack and Karen, student loan debt has become a major burden on tens of millions of Americans. Debt robs us of the freedom to make choices.

According to the text, what is the current volume of student loan debt owed by Americans? How many borrowers are there? What is the average amount of student loan debt a young person carries entering the workforce?

_____

_____

_____

_____

Do you or anyone in your family still owe on student loans? If so, how much do you owe and what is your plan for repaying them?

_____

_____

_____

_____

Entrepreneurship is not a purely American phenomenon, but the United States is generally considered the most successful entrepreneurial country in the world. Roughly half of all jobs created in our economy are created and maintained by small to medium businesses. These diligent and productive members of society, who become business owners and heads of successful corporations, create wealth through long hours, hard work, and risk-taking. I call them "makers." An indication of this is that the 2017 GDP of the United States of $19.3 trillion is a three hundred-fold increase over the GDP of $59.7 billion in 1917.

Yet, these same people are often portrayed as greedy or exploitative robber barons. At the same time, society elevates the unproductive and lackadaisical members of society as victims. These people feel that they are entitled. I call them "takers."

We should be elevating the "makers" who create wealth and jobs through hard work, not the "takers" who accept a job and then deliver the bare minimum effort to get by. Taking in this way is another form of stealing.

How do you feel about capitalism and entrepreneurship? Have you started a business or owned your own business? Describe your experience.

_____

_____

_____

_____

How about the other side of this spectrum? When you see people who do the minimum and feel entitled, how does that make you feel?

_____

_____

_____

_____

Key Quotes:

"Most of our decisions are rooted in emotion, rather than logic. That is certainly true where spending decisions are concerned."

"Addiction to buying is a very real thing."

"Piling up debt today that you presume you'll be able to pay with money you expect to earn in the future is essentially running a Ponzi scam on yourself."

"What many Christians don't realize is that spending money you don't have is a form of stealing. It's stealing from your future. And from your family's future."

"This explains why debt is so insidious. Borrowing kills hope."

CHAPTER NINE

GREAT GAIN

Long before anyone was *Keeping Up with the Kardashians*, people were "keeping up with the Joneses." This popular cartoon strip appeared for over two decades in the early twentieth century and became an icon that poked fun at how people like Mrs. McGinnis constantly strove to buy things in a desperate effort to be something they weren't.

The popularity of this cartoon grew in conjunction with several factors from that era, including the ability to print and cheaply mail consumer magazines, the array of new products and technologies being brought to market as the industrial age of America matured, and the steadily increasing population growth during this period. Advertising was coming of age.

Millennia before either the Joneses or Kardashians, however, a similar and more historic event took place:

> Now the whole earth had one language and one speech. And it came to pass, as they journeyed from the east, that they found a plain in the land of Shinar, and they dwelt there. Then they said to one another, "Come, let us make bricks and bake them thoroughly." They had brick for stone, and they had asphalt for mortar. And they said, "Come, let us build ourselves a city, and

a tower whose top is in the heavens; let us make a name for ourselves, lest we be scattered abroad over the face of the whole earth."

But the LORD came down to see the city and the tower which the sons of men had built. And the LORD said, "Indeed the people are one and they all have one language, and this is what they begin to do; now nothing that they propose to do will be withheld from them. Come, let Us go down and there confuse their language, that they may not understand one another's speech." So the LORD scattered them abroad from there over the face of all the earth, and they ceased building the city. Therefore its name is called Babel, because there the LORD confused the language of all the earth; and from there the LORD scattered them abroad over the face of all the earth. (Genesis 11:1–9)

This event came about not because of advertising, but because the families of the sons of Noah decided that they wanted to have a family reunion, "make a name for [themselves.]" (v. 4), and establish a city to keep the family together. Ostensibly, that was the reason.

The true motivation behind that tower, however, was not to simply establish a family compound. It was far more sinister. The descendants of Noah wanted to "keep up with" the wealthiest and most powerful King—their own Creator. If they were to keep up, they knew they had to reach all the way up to the King's "castle"—the heavens.

Read Isaiah 14:12–15 and Revelation 12:1–12. What do you think the motivation was behind the troubling figure described in these passages? What was Satan's relationship with God before he was cast out (see Ezekiel 28:13)?

_____

_____

_____

_____

Why do you want something that you don't have? Something new? Perhaps something that you don't need? The simple answer is that in your heart you are not content with what you already have or the situation that you are in.

In 1 Timothy 6:6 the apostle Paul directly proclaims the power of contentment: "Now godliness with contentment is great gain." Besides money, what might Paul include in a list of things that are "great gain"?

_____

_____

_____

_____

According to the text, "When you combine godliness—that is, putting God first in your priorities—with contentment, you gain _____. You gain _____. You gain _____. Above all, you gain _____."

If you are not content, of course, then you are discontent. You are a prisoner to your cravings and destined for disappointment.

Besides the biblical references and the example we saw with Andy, we frequently see this human condition dealt with in secular literature.

John Steinbeck published his last novel, *The Winter of our Discontent*, in 1961. Ethan Allen Hawley, the protagonist in Steinbeck's novel, personifies in stark terms the conflict between corruption and integrity among Hawley, his family, friends, and business associates.

Andy, who made the trip to Angola in chapter six, and Ethan Hawley had the same problem. They both focused on what other people had and allowed into their hearts the primary enemy of discontentment: *comparison*. And comparison can lead us down the slippery slope to resentment, envy, and pride.

Prior to his trip to Angola, what comparisons was Andy making in his life? How did his Angola experience change the way he viewed his situation?

_____

_____

Comparison, by scoring and evaluating every person, circumstance, and possession, tends to result in a binary judgment that something of mine is better or worse than something else. It can feed a sense of insecurity or pride, and it creates contention with others. It opens the door to one of the ugliest sins of all—envy. Envy was what motivated the religious leaders in Jesus' day to have Him crucified:

> But Pilate answered them, saying, "Do you want me to release to you the King of the Jews?" For he knew that the chief priests had handed Him over *because of envy.* (Mark 15:9–10, emphasis added)

What things do you tend to notice or tempt you most about others or your surroundings? Give some specific examples. Why do you think that those things (or situations) are a source of comparison for you?

_____

_____

_____

_____

Has some situation of comparison ever become a source of contention with another person? Explain.

_____

_____

_____

_____

Another inevitable consequence of comparison is anger and resentment toward God. It's easy to blame God for the fact that your neighbor *seems* to be doing better. Of course, you don't know what is going on in that neighbor's home or his soul—there could be great pain and despair.

Have you ever looked at another person's things or circumstances and admired them to the point of feeling angry or ungrateful to God? In other words, did you find yourself in contention with God? How did you deal with that feeling at the time? Explain.

_____

_____

_____

_____

Read Mark 15:9–10. What particularly ugly sin, prompted by Satan himself, grows out of the spirit of comparison? According to Hebrews 12:1, whose race (path or life) are you supposed to run and focus on?

_____

_____

_____

_____

God created you to pursue the plan and the path that He created *for you*! This was a problem even for Peter when he compared himself with John:

> Peter, seeing him, said to Jesus, "But Lord, what about this man?"
> Jesus said to him, "If I will that he remain till I come, what is that to you? You follow Me." (John 21:21–22)

Jesus basically told Peter: "Run your race. And let John run his." Joy comes from finding your true purpose, not from carnal pleasure—not from whatever you want.

The opposite of contentment is covetousness. Comparison is the tool the enemy uses to stimulate pride and anger in the heart. Covetousness is the

deadly habit of craving what someone else possesses. It is also the focus of
the tenth commandment:

> You shall not covet your neighbor's house; you shall not covet
> your neighbor's wife, nor his male servant, nor his female servant,
> nor his ox, nor his donkey, nor anything that is your neighbor's.
> (Exodus 20:17)

Jesus also warned His disciples about the danger:

> And He said to them, "Take heed and beware of covetousness, for
> one's life does not consist in the abundance of the things he pos-
> sesses." (Luke 12:15)

Read Luke 12:15 in the New Living Translation. Considering all these
warnings, state in your own words how you *should* measure your life.

_____

_____

_____

_____

According to Colossians 3:5, what is coveting? Explain why Paul defines
it as such.

_____

_____

_____

_____

> Let your conduct be without covetousness; be content with such
> things as you have. For He Himself has said, "I will never leave
> you nor forsake you." (Hebrews 13:5)

This verse clearly contrasts contentment and coveting. Why does God offer this promise to never forsake you? What is He saying about comparison, insecurity, and significance in this simple verse?

_____

_____

_____

_____

God said He would never forsake me. Yet, Jesus cried out on the cross asking why God had forsaken Him (see Matthew 27:46). The reality is that God *did* forsake Jesus at that moment. God did forsake Him so that He would never forsake us. As Jesus bore our sins so we could receive His righteousness, Jesus bore our rejection so we could receive God's acceptance.

Why, based on this promise and Jesus' sacrifice, can we be content rather than covetous?

_____

_____

_____

_____

No possession, no achievement, no position, and no person can fulfill the deepest longings of your heart. God loves to bless His children, including satisfying them with material things in this life (see Psalm 103:2–5), but first He wants to be sure that our hearts and desires are set on eternal things.

God commanded Adam and Eve to be fruitful, multiply, and have dominion over the earth. He wants us to provide increase by *stewarding well* whatever blessings He entrusts to us. That means we must aspire to *become* or *build* something, as opposed to lusting to have something.

Reread the story in this chapter of the man I mentioned who achieved his goal of being financially independent by the age of forty.

What was the result of that worldly achievement? How did it affect him? How did the man break free from the misery his achievement caused?

_____

_____

_____

_____

Consider the man's quote: "If your goal is to climb to the top, there is only one thing left to do when you reach your goal. Jump off. There is nowhere else to climb." Read the proclamation of Noah's descendants from Genesis 11:4: "And they said, 'Come, let us build ourselves a city, and a tower whose top is in the heavens; let us make a name for ourselves, lest we be scattered abroad over the face of the whole earth.'"

Compare the sentiments from these two passages. What were the consequences of their words? What is the Lord saying to you about "climbing to the top"?

_____

_____

_____

_____

According to the text, what are the two reasons that contentment is a source of great gain?

_____

_____

Describe what it means to you when God says, "Why would you covet what someone else has when you have Me?"

_____

_____

_____

_____

Key Quotes:

"When you combine "godliness"—that is, putting God first in your priorities—with contentment, you gain peace. You gain confidence. You gain security. Above all, you gain freedom."

"Comparison is also a sin because it invariably produces anger and resentment toward God."

"Comparison opens the door to one of the ugliest sins of all—envy."

"When you focus on someone else's situation, you take the focus off of God's plan for your life."

"When you allow covetousness to destroy your sense of contentment, you make what you're coveting a false God."

"Material things are temporary, fleeting, prone to rust, decay, and deterioration. In contrast, the things of God are eternal."

CHAPTER TEN

THE WITNESS STAND

You are being watched. All the time.

A recent television series portrays a scenario in which the government has deployed a secret system that watches everyone all the time. The designer of this sophisticated system, which uses artificial intelligence, sold it to the government. The system was designed to prevent terrorism, and the government doesn't care about ordinary people. The designer does care about people, however, so he uses a back door to the system to help solve other crimes. They are watching everyone. All the time.

One interesting facet of this show is that there are two different motivations for the use of the system. The government is only interested in terrorism. It is not interested in ordinary cases involving ordinary people, regardless of the nature of the crime. The designer, of course, has the opposite motivation, which is why he built a back-door system to get information that the government "discards" about ordinary people. What the system provides, however, is information about potential future crimes, which the designer and his team try to prevent.

When the user gets information from the system, it is just in the form of a Social Security number, and it is often difficult to tell if the person selected will be a victim or perpetrator. Nevertheless, one is being watched.

All the time. And a person being watched is, according to the title of the program, a *Person of Interest.*

How would you feel if your privacy were being invaded as this television show depicts? Do you feel similarly about red light cameras being used to catch traffic violators?

_____

_____

_____

_____

The driver of the poorly maintained car that passed me on the freeway was probably focused on where he (or she) was going and what would happen when he got there. Nevertheless, as the driver went down the road, he should have been aware that, regardless of where he was going or what he was going to do, he was also fulfilling another function:

Now then, we are ambassadors for Christ. (2 Corinthians 5:20)

An ambassador, of course, can range from an official representative of a country to an unofficial representative of any organization. The *purpose* of an ambassador is to model the characteristics or principles that the organization represents, with the intent to develop good relationships between organizations or between the organization and the public. An ambassador expects that everyone is watching. All the time (see Matthew 5:16).

What does it mean to you to be an ambassador for Christ? Have you thought of this witnessing as something that happens only when you are actively representing Jesus and the Church?

_____

_____

_____

_____

_____

Like in the television show, the world is watching how God's people live their lives. All the time.

God considers everyone who is watching you to be your "neighbor." The Old Testament laws dealt with how to live righteously with neighbors. How much more would God want His chosen people to live well among them today? Jesus taught us to "love your neighbor as yourself" (Matt. 22:39).

Why does God want us to treat our neighbors well? Why does He want us to go beyond kindness and *love* them, too?

_____

_____

_____

_____

Based on Jesus' response to the Pharisee in Luke 10—the story of the Good Samaritan—who does Jesus say our neighbor is?

_____

_____

_____

_____

Your life witnesses to everyone you meet, and does so in various ways. How you handle your money and resources is an important reflection. I'm not talking about your level of affluence, as is made clear in this well-known story:

> Jesus sat opposite the treasury and saw how the people put money into the treasury. And many who were rich put in much. Then one poor widow came and threw in two mites, which make a quadrans. So He called His disciples to Himself and said to them, "Assuredly, I say to you that this poor widow has put in more than all those who have given to the treasury; for they all put in out of their abundance, but she out of her poverty put in all that she had, her whole livelihood." (Mark 12:40–44)

Every action you take—every day—is a living witness to your neighbors. It does not matter what resources you have.

The widow in this story was poor. How do you imagine she was dressed—not just *what* she was wearing, but what about the condition of her clothes? How did she likely interact with the others at the treasury? How did she speak with and treat others?

_____

_____

_____

_____

When you manage your money wisely, peace and power will shine through and reflect positively on the cause of Christ.

Good stewardship also empowers you with another powerful way of showing the goodness of God.

> I have shown you in every way, by laboring like this, that you must support the weak. And remember the words of the Lord Jesus, that He said, "It is more blessed to give than to receive." (Acts 20:35)

The Greek word here means "happy." Much of my previous book, *The Blessed Life*, was built around the truth that a life of generosity is a happy life.

If the happiest, most joy-filled life one can experience is one of generosity, how happy was the widow who gave the two mites?

_____

_____

_____

_____

Of course, generosity borne of good stewardship must be the province of both those who have little and those who have much. That same spirit of generosity the widow showed in Jesus' time was what prompted Debbie and me to bless that family of six at the diner during our motorcycle trip to the mountains a few years ago.

I am sure we experienced the same kind of joy, regardless of the amount of money given.

God created us for good works such as these.

> Let your light so shine before men, that they may see your good works and glorify your Father in heaven. (Matthew 5:16)

These good works have no effect on our salvation, but they have tremendous influence on other people by pointing them to God, and they bring great joy to the good steward who does them. That is why God is always watching. Each of us is a *Person of Interest*. We are always on the witness stand.

Key Quotes:

"Jesus' story reveals that your 'neighbor' is anyone you happen to come into contact with in your daily life. . . . What kind of story is your life telling to those with whom you interact?"

"When you manage your finances wisely . . . the peace and power that shine through your life reflect positively on the cause of Christ."

"The happiest, most fulfilling, most joy-filled life you can experience is a life of generosity."

"Your 'good works' have no bearing on your salvation or how much God loves you. But your good works do have an impact on others. They shine as a light for people in darkness. Your generosity points them to God."

CHAPTER ELEVEN

AIM BEFORE YOU SHOOT

Not that I have already attained, or am already perfected; but I press on, that I may lay hold of that for which Christ Jesus has also laid hold of me. Brethren, I do not count myself to have apprehended; but one thing I do, forgetting those things which are behind and reaching forward to those things which are ahead, I press toward the goal for the prize of the upward call of God in Christ Jesus. (Philippians 3:12–14)

A recent Google search for "goal setting" drew 446 million results in just over half a second. The apostle Paul succinctly stated his approach to goal setting for the believer in just seventy-seven words. The power of setting tangible, measurable, achievable goals is a biblical practice mentioned throughout the Scripture.

As I showed in the examples from my junior high school basketball days and my son's motorcycle safety class, goal setting is a learned process. Two general pitfalls await us if we are not careful.

The first is when we focus on an obstacle (physical or otherwise) that is immediately in front of us. We can focus so much on the obstacle (like my son did) that our ability to properly consider the path and respond is compromised.

The second pitfall is to focus on a prize without considering anything else. We might call this either obsessive-compulsive behavior or daydreaming, depending on our personality. Either way, we become so caught up in the singular goal (as I did) that we are again unable to marshal the proper resources or account for the obstacles that will inevitably come our way.

Can you remember a time when you faced an obstacle (physical, emotional, relational, or otherwise) that you focused on so much that you could not get around it? What did you do to eventually overcome the obstacle? What did you learn from that?

_____

_____

_____

_____

_____

Can you remember a time when you daydreamed about something so much that you obsessed and either were unable to decide what to do or failed to see the challenges that would be in your path?

_____

_____

_____

_____

Two key basic principles to help you in goal setting are found in Scripture. Read Proverbs 16:3 and 29:18.

Proverbs 16:3 says that the Lord will establish your plans when you commit your strivings and goals to Him. Goal setting is easier when you commit your activities to the Lord because the Lord is on your team!

Proverbs 29:18 emphasizes the importance of vision. Vision to the believer means that we have light—because Jesus is the light (see Psalm 119:105 and John 8:12). Jesus is the Word and a light for our path. Our vision is also clearer because of the guidance of the Holy Spirit (see Romans 8:14).

When you first think about a major decision or action, do you pray about it and commit it to the Lord?

_____

_____

_____

_____

How does the Word of God help you in decision-making or planning? Have you sought out and heard from the Holy Spirit when considering your decisions or plans?

_____

_____

_____

_____

The power of goal setting is also well documented in the worlds of business and behavioral science. Numerous studies, such as the one I draw on from Dominican University, validate the benefits of a proper approach to goal setting, as do the numerous examples of successful individuals.

Our goal for this chapter is to give you the knowledge and the tools to craft achievable financial goals and begin developing a strategy to achieve them. There are several steps.

Where Are You?

The goal is the end point. In order to create the path to get to the end point, you must know the starting point—where you are now. For a trip to Denver, you might want to drive or fly. There will be different routes, methods of travel, and obstacles for the two options. Regardless of the route, however, the trip will start from your house. When it comes to financial goals, you will need to determine your current situation as related to assets, debt, income, and expenditures.

We go into much greater detail about gathering and using financial information in chapter thirteen about budgeting. However, you will have to know where to go to get that financial information and make sure that you are able to properly process it.

Do you keep detailed financial records? Do you balance your checkbook regularly? Who in your household is primarily responsible for financial decisions and record keeping?

_____

_____

_____

_____

It is important to keep good financial records and keep those records organized. Record keeping requirements may differ depending on whether you work strictly for a salary or own a business. Different types of businesses will have additional requirements. Regardless of the complexity of your finances, begin right now to review the way you keep and manage financial records.

Where Do You Want to Go?

Remember that I said earlier how it is easy to focus on an obstacle or end up daydreaming about an unreasonable goal. (In other words, the goal of winning a billion-dollar lottery prize or inheriting a fortune from a long-lost relative doesn't count.) There are several steps to take in your goal setting process.

Begin with prayer. Pray in faith. Heed the wisdom in James 1:5–6. Remember, He will never leave or forsake you and His Holy Spirit will guide you—if you will let Him.

Do you regularly pray and ask for guidance about important decisions in your life? If not, why not? How has God responded to those prayers?

_____

_____

_____

_____

Second, your goals must proceed from your heart and vision. They should be based on your values and not made to impress others. This is *your* goal.

Do you currently have good awareness and understanding of your heart and vision (and those of your spouse if you're married)? Explain. If the answer is no, you might want to engage in some soul-searching and self-evaluation (again, with your spouse if you're married) about your spiritual situation. Write down your thoughts.

_____

_____

_____

_____

Third, your goals should be measurable and specific.

The easiest way to approach this issue is to ask, "How much, by when?" Include as much detail as is reasonably possible. Lose weight is quite general; lose ten pounds is more specific and measurable, but "weigh one hundred and sixty pounds at nine o'clock on October 1" is even clearer.

Consider some goals you have set in the past. Have they been measurable and specific? Give some examples and discuss how they were or were not. If they weren't, how could they have been stated better? Also, considering one or more of those goals, describe how whether you made them specific and measurable—or not—contributed to achieving them.

_____

_____

_____

For a number of reasons, your goals will evolve and change over time. Be willing to review and evaluate them as circumstances change, and change them if necessary.

Describe some situations where you changed a goal after you set it. What caused the change and how did you approach revising the goal?

_____

_____

_____

_____

How Long Will It Take to Get There?

Goals should be ambitious enough to challenge you, but also attainable. They should be reasonable.

Yes, God can do miracles, but our plan of action cannot depend on that possibility. Remember what I said about the "daydreamer" approach to goals. Simply waiting for a miracle is not consistent with a God that rewards diligent obedience and hard work. (Read Ecclesiastes 9:10 and 2 Thessalonians 3:10.)

It will also help to break down your big goals into smaller, incremental goals or objectives. This makes it easier to monitor your progress and also reduces the stress of trying to do too much at one time. Every long journey begins with a single step.

Have you ever daydreamed about a miracle? Are you prone to being more of a dreamer or a doer? Do you tend to be hesitant to start something?

_____

_____

_____

_____

_____

Write the Vision

The Dominican University study also validated that people who write down their goals are more likely to follow them through to completion. Paul kept his goal before him. He didn't have a cell phone or computer screen saver to remind him. But I would almost bet that if we searched Paul's prison cell in Rome, we would have found some notes that reminded him of the prize he so diligently sought.

Do you tend to write down your goals? Give some examples of goals that you did write down and some that you did not.

_____

_____

_____

_____

Make an Action Plan

Finally, as the old saying goes, "Plan your work and work your plan." The specifics of the goal and how you will measure success will lead you to distinct actions. That journey of a thousand miles (or ten) will contain many steps, which you will need to take in a certain order. I will introduce you to some practical tools to help you do that.

What tools have you used in the past to organize your projects or activities? These could be as complex as using a project management software program on the job, or as simple as making a list on paper.

_____

_____

_____

_____

_____

Add Accountability and Assistance

It is wise to let someone outside your household know what your plan is and ask them to monitor your actions.

The Dominican study validated the benefits of accountability. But this is probably something every one of us already knows is necessary.

People who know they are being watched act differently. But the Bible also tells us to be accountable and in community with others. Gateway Church has apostolic elders who provide broad oversight of the church's activities, and to whom the eldership can go for advice on important issues. Throughout the Gateway Church staff, we have a regular program of communication and oversight.

There is no reason to be ashamed of needing help. When we are sick, we go to a doctor. There are many Christian stewardship resources available to help you.

What avenues of accountability do you have in your life now? Are you a member of a small group or home group? List some people you might ask to pray for you and help you with goal setting.

_____

_____

_____

_____

Key Quotes:

"The first thing the teacher taught them was, 'Look where you *want* to go, not where you're currently going.'"

"A focus on goals is a vital key to getting where we want to go in life and in God."

"You're not on your own here! God is your eager and powerful partner in this endeavor to align your life with His wisdom and ways. Involve Him in every facet."

"There is great wisdom in having a person or persons outside your household who know what you've committed to do and what your plan is."

CHAPTER TWELVE

HEARSES DON'T PULL U-HAULS

You may have already heard the story of Steve Dulin, which I related anonymously in my book *The Blessed Life*. In that context I described how, when he responded in faith to God's call to increase his giving, he was mightily blessed. The increase in giving, as I said, was done out of his heart, and God trusted him to be faithful with His financial blessing.

I don't recommend you try to replicate what Steve did, since He was specifically instructed by God to do so.

However, there is more to the story. Besides asking Steve to give more, He also asked him to get out of debt and start saving more. That certainly made the circumstances of God's instructions more interesting!

In chapter four I mentioned that good stewards do three things: They (1) spend wisely, (2) save, and (3) give. The giving part was covered clearly in God's promise to Steve. When you understand that a key element of "spending wisely" is not carrying unsecured debt, you will see that God's instructions are a road map for good stewardship.

Have you ever heard instructions from God, either quite directly or as a still small voice? In what other ways has God instructed you? Explain.

_____

_____

_____

_____

_____

The Dulins stepped out in obedience by adjusting their lifestyle and budget to do all three things God had instructed them to do. They started by paying off their low-interest student loan debt, using funds from investments that paid a higher return. Again, this was counterintuitive (and criticized by some well-meaning friends), but they were being obedient to God's commands. They then began to pay off their home mortgage.

The Dulins started with their tithe, then prayed about the amount they were supposed to save and put against debt each month. God gave them a specific figure. Once they had all three figures, the amount left after taking that from their income became their living expenses.

Do you think God would have blessed the Dulins the same way if they had increased their lifestyle and expenses as their income increased? Why or why not?

_____

_____

_____

_____

You can become a stewardship story like the Dulins. The key is being willing to live below your means.

As I mentioned before, hoping to win the lottery or inherit a fortune will not be the answer. The answer is simply to adjust your lifestyle so that your income consistently exceeds your outgo. The principle is *simple*, but that doesn't mean it's easy.

At this time, does your income exceed your outgo? In other words, are you spending more than you earn? How do they compare?

_____

_____

_____

_____

The secret to living within and below your means is to *trust* in God—to trust that He is always with us and that He will take care of us like he takes care of all of His creation.

When we live above our means, we don't typically spend a great deal more; we usually just steal a little from our future selves. God would prefer you to live *well below* your means—as Steve and Melody did, with extraordinary results.

Why is it so hard to live like that? When we go back to the passage we looked at earlier in 1 Timothy 6, we see one of the reasons. Verse 7 says, "For we brought nothing into this world, and it is certain we can carry nothing out." That's why a friend of mine says that you've never seen a hearse pulling a U-Haul.

That is, unless you were an early Egyptian. A number of primitive civilizations, most notably the Egyptians, did believe in an afterlife and a need for material goods there. Many tombs have been endowed with grave goods that included everything from gold and silver to food and clothing. This is, of course, the opposite of Jesus' teaching. You and I will take the same possessions into eternity as Bill Gates and Warren Buffett.

Our passage from Paul's letter to Timothy goes on to say:

And having food and clothing, with these we shall be content. But those who desire to be rich fall into temptation and a snare, and into many foolish and harmful lusts which drown men in destruction and perdition. For the love of money is a root of all kinds of evil, for which some have strayed from the faith in their greediness, and pierced themselves through with many sorrows. (1 Timothy 6:8–10)

How would you honestly describe your heart attitude toward money and wealth? Is your journey through this book helping adjust your outlook?

_____

_____

As we learned earlier, looking to riches as a source of happiness is a form of idolatry. Paul says it can "drown men in destruction and perdition."

Learning to live below your means goes back to *learning* to be content. As Paul said,

> I am not saying this because I am in need, for I have learned to be content whatever the circumstances. I know what it is to be in need, and I know what it is to have plenty. I have learned the secret of being content in any and every situation, whether well fed or hungry, whether living in plenty or in want. I can do all this through him who gives me strength. (Philippians 4:11–13 NIV)

Contentment comes from within you. It is an attitude and posture of the heart.

Many people try to appear wealthier than they are, while some very wealthy individuals live simply, and you'd never know they were rich. What Solomon pointed out in Proverbs 13:7 still applies today. Sam Walton drove around in a 1979 Ford pickup truck until the day he died. Even Warren Buffett still lives in the relatively modest home that he bought for $31,500 in 1958. He once said that he is happy there, and if he thought he would be happier somewhere else, he would move. (In context, understand that Buffett is a self-professed agnostic. That doesn't make the sentiment any less valid.)

We often consider what it would be like to meet and talk with other people—such as Bible figures or famous people—when we get to heaven. What would you ask them about their views of money and prosperity?

Envy and greed will constantly feed off each other. People who desire to have things in order to be envied by others will then find, as Ecclesiastes 5:10 says, "He who loves silver will not be satisfied with silver; nor he who loves abundance, with increase."

With what one or two specific things (or people and circumstances) do you struggle about envy? How have you tried to deal with them?

Key Quotes:

"The key to Steve Dulin's amazing stewardship testimony will also be the key to yours.... The willingness to live below your means."

"Warren Buffett and Bill Gates will take the same amount of material wealth into eternity as you and I will. That is, precisely none."

"If you want to live below your means, the most important thing you can do is learn to be content."

"When you're an envious person, you begin to want to be envied by others.... What a low and ugly motivation for living."

CHAPTER THIRTEEN

HELLO, MR. BUDGET

Math. Just the word strikes fear in the hearts of many young people and adults. It seems like older generations are more likely than young people today to be able to manipulate numbers, perhaps because we were raised in a time when there were fewer options. Before computers, we had simple calculators; but as recently as the 1960s, engineers still used slide rules for calculations. Slide rules were carried by astronauts on the Apollo space missions.

The reasons can be debated, but the United States has consistently ranked poorly in mathematics compared to much of the world:

> The math achievement of American high school students in 2015 fell for the second time in a row on a major international benchmark, pushing the United States down to the bottom half of 72 nations and regions around the world who participate in the international test, known as the Program for International Student Assessment or PISA. Among the 35 industrialized nations that are members of the Organization for Economic Cooperation and Development (OECD), the U.S. now ranks 31st.[7]

Perhaps we can now have a bit more sympathy for—or at least a better understanding of—the poor drive-through cashier who had difficulty calculating the change for my food order. Of course, the stakes are higher and more precise calculations are required in other circumstances, as anyone familiar with the aborted Apollo 13 moon mission will remember.

How proficient are you at basic mathematics? Can you easily calculate numbers in your head? Can you readily use a calculator?

_____

_____

_____

_____

By way of review, there are three things excellent stewards do: commit to spend wisely, save diligently, and give generously. Then the good steward sets goals in those areas.

Simple mathematics is the foundation for good budgeting. (Jesus himself warned against the casual approach to math in Luke 14:28–31.) Fortunately, the budget is a simple, time-tested tool that we can use to help manage our finances.

Do you currently have a household budget? How do you and your family approach the budget? If you are married, how do you and your spouse compare in terms of being frugal vs. being a spender?

_____

_____

_____

_____

Gateway Church has an active stewardship ministry to help our members budget and achieve financial goals. What resources do you use when considering budgeting or financial planning?

_____

_____

_____

_____

What are the six benefits of having a budget?

_____

_____

_____

_____

_____

I have cited in this chapter numerous resources and tools that are available to help you create and manage a budget. If you do have a budget, what tools do you use to create and keep track of your budget?

_____

_____

_____

_____

There are four main steps to building and sticking to a budget.

Courageously Evaluate Your Current Situation

This is the first and often the most difficult step, especially if there are family members involved or the financial situation is precarious. Nonetheless, *denial* is not an option. Breaking the addiction to bad financial management is like breaking any other addiction. You must face the truth and identify every debt and every asset. In business terms, this is your balance sheet.

What does the balance between your debts and assets look like at this time?

_____

_____

_____

_____

Review Your Income and Spending

This step requires some more consideration. Your income may be quite steady or may fluctuate. If you have a variable income stream, you will have to make some assumptions about the timing and amount of your income. Be conservative in your assumptions.

Describe your income stream. If it is variable, what must you take into consideration to come up with a workable regular income for budgeting purposes? Is your business cyclical? Are you commissioned on sales? Is your income heavily reliant on tips?

_____

_____

_____

_____

Expenses can be categorized in several ways:

- mandatory or discretionary
- fixed or variable
- monthly or periodic

While expenses are what they are, sometimes you can adjust the categories. A variable expense like utility costs can sometimes be set up on an averaging plan with the utility company. A periodic expense like car and homeowner's insurance can often be paid over a period of months, though usually at a slightly higher charge.

Identify Values and Goals

We already considered goals in chapter eleven, and as we saw in chapter five, good stewards put first things first.

The story from Stephen Covey's book about the time management seminar of MBA students reminds us that we might not always be able to readily determine what the truly *important* things are. Be mindful of the truly important things that Covey calls the "big rocks."

When it comes to money and budget, make your *firstfruits* a priority. God must be the first of your "first things," which means budgeting your tithe first.

Pray (with your spouse if married) about the idea of firstfruits in your budget. What is the Holy Spirit saying to you about your tithe? About priorities for your budget in general?

_____

_____

_____

_____

_____

Plan to Save

The final key step to budget building is the second "big rock"—setting aside something for savings every month.

We looked at five general categories for savings: emergencies, needs, wants, the future (retirement), and giving.

Consider the two categories of needs and wants. Again, if you are married, discuss with your spouse. What things do you have a hard time deciding which category they belong in? Explain.

_____

_____

_____

_____

_____

Read Proverbs 6:6 and Proverbs 3:9–10 again. How important do you consider the ability to give over and above your tithe?

_____

_____

_____

_____

What are the two basic stewardship principles to keep in mind as you take part in this process?

_____

_____

_____

_____

After saving, we move on to expenses. The biggest and most difficult issue for most people is dealing with discretionary expenses. Just like when you set aside savings for needs and wants, you will have to make decisions about expenses. What parts of your lifestyle are truly *essential*? The only way that you can do this is to be brutally honest and reduce discretionary expenses until the net is less than your income. It may well be painful. However, if you keep your eyes on the prize and are truly committed to good stewardship, God will respond with heavenly help.

There are a number of methods you can use to help in the process of following your budget. Many people are still comfortable with the use of checks and cash. Electronic tools are available to help you monitor your spending and even help classify it. What is your method of choice for monitoring your expenses and following your budget? Why?

_____

_____

_____

_____

Key Quotes:

"In a sense, budgeting is just spending ALL your money in accordance with your goals."

"Whatever your goals are, you won't get there by accident. . . . A budget that reflects these values and goals is your road map."

"Having a budget takes the emotional factor out of spending decisions."

"Your firm commitment to become a faithful steward will be met with heavenly help."

CHAPTER FOURTEEN

TO DEBT, OR NOT TO DEBT

In chapter eight I warned against financing things you cannot afford, comparing that practice to a Ponzi scheme on yourself that steals from your own future. However, that does not mean that I am against all debt in all circumstances.

Debt has been around in some form for thousands of years. Archaeologists still discover small ceramic "debt pods" throughout the region of ancient Mesopotamia. These pods memorialized the agreement to repay someone for the purchase of a good prior to the establishment of a currency. Two traders were not likely to be carrying around the exact quantity of barley and olive oil that each would agree to pay for the other's product.

Likewise, passages such as Leviticus 25 and Deuteronomy 15 provide biblical teaching about lending. Verse 6 of Deuteronomy 15 is a prophecy teaching about the blessing that will come if His people will keep His commandments. It also indicates that it may be necessary and beneficial to help the poor out from time to time.

By the way, you will notice in Deuteronomy 15:1 that God commands all lenders to grant a release of debt every seven years to their neighbor or brother (their fellow Israelite), but *not* to any foreigners. Finally, in Leviticus chapter 25, we read that the Year of Jubilee (fiftieth year, see vv. 8–13) was also a year when debt was to be released. There was clearly lending and borrowing happening in those days, the parameters of which were established by the Lord.

Deuteronomy 15 proclaims a year of release from debt for fellow Israelites every seven years. Deuteronomy 15:9 says, "Beware lest there be a wicked thought in your heart, saying, 'The seventh year, the year of release, is at hand,' and your eye be evil against your poor brother and you give him nothing, and he cry out to the LORD against you, and it become sin among you." What does this verse warn against? Explain.

_____

_____

_____

_____

In the New Testament, Romans 13:8, which reads, "Owe no one anything except to love one another, for he who loves another has fulfilled the law," is often cited as prohibition against debt. However, this verse uses the word debt in the sense of wrongdoing, as in the King James Version's language of the Lord's Prayer: "Forgive us our debts, as we forgive our debtors" (Matt. 6:12). In a practical sense, it is impossible to *never* owe *anything* to *anybody*. The real issue is how to use wisely whatever debt is reasonable and acceptable.

Read Psalm 37:21. What does this verse imply about debt?

_____

_____

_____

_____

Debt is also an important issue for businesses. During the 1970s through the early 2000s, many investors acquired companies in a transaction known as a leveraged buyout (LBO). Times were good, so investors would put up a small amount of equity (often less than 10 percent) and finance the remainder with debt, expecting the long-term cash flow to cover the debt and interest payments. That is the principle of leverage. Does that sound familiar? It's just like when we borrow from our own future. And the results can be equally bad.

An example of one well-known company has been in the news recently. In 2018, Toys "R" Us filed for bankruptcy. *Bloomberg Businessweek* talks of the real issue, fueled by $5 billion in debt from an LBO:

> Online competition was inevitable, *but debt is what did it in.*
>
> The overarching problem was costs—and importantly, *interest expense on borrowings.* By 2007, just before the financial crisis hit, *the retailer's interest expense spiked to 97 percent of its operating profit....* While LBOs of the size of Toys "R" Us are rarely done these days, *debt has become the payment of choice* for some megamergers between companies in industries ranging from telecommunications to health care. We may be out of the woods in terms of overloaded LBOs, but we've added a new risk at an entirely new magnitude. (emphasis added)[8]

Remember our *Shark Tank* folks? Very often one of the companies will sound like a good investment until they reveal that they have already incurred a great deal of debt to grow their business. The savvy sharks almost always pass on those debt-laden enterprises.

Credit Cards

With credit card debt in America exceeding a trillion dollars—more than five times the GDP of Angola—there is clearly a problem. The danger is twofold. First, the interest rates on credit cards are exorbitant, often exceeding 20 percent. Second, credit standards for lending have often been quite low, which makes it that much easier to get in over one's head.

However, having one or two credit cards and paying off the balances in full every month can be beneficial, for several reasons:

- It is almost a necessity when traveling (try renting a car without one).
- Having a credit card helps build good credit if you ever do want to finance a house or car.
- Many credit cards today come with cash back features that can actually add to your income. You can buy many things and pay a majority of bills without any additional fee and receive a rebate of anywhere from 1 percent to 5 percent back from the credit card company. For example, using a card that pays 2 percent back on $3,000 worth of payments per month creates an additional $60 of monthly income. The credit card company (often a bank) is actually paying *you* interest. That can be good stewardship.

How many credit cards do you have? Do you have balances that you do not pay off each month? What is the interest rate on those balances? What is the Holy Spirit prompting you to do about that credit card debt?

_____

_____

_____

_____

_____

If you have accrued a substantial amount of unsecured debt through credit cards, consider consolidating and refinancing them at a lower rate. However, that would *only* be acceptable if you can manage your cash flow without having to build up a balance again and have a plan to stick to that.

Once you have gotten out from under the lifestyle of debt, there are three key concepts to apply when considering whether to incur debt.

First, consider if there is another way to get what you need without taking on debt. Can you liquidate assets to pay with cash? Perhaps you can borrow something from someone for a while rather than buying a new thing. Be creative. Make debt the option of last resort.

What are some other potential creative options that you might be able to use to avoid unsecured debt?

_____

_____

_____

_____

_____

Second, formulate an escape plan. You might leave a high-return investment account in place while entering into a low-interest loan. Or perhaps, as was the case with the car for my daughter Elaine, the cost of borrowing is cheaper, so long as you've made sure it's the better financial decision.

Third, "Do the math." Evaluate the numbers. If this is difficult for you, ask for help. You don't have to do it on your own. The examples in this chapter can provide some ideas.

Making wise financial decisions often boils down to getting answers to three basic questions. Fill in the blanks:

- Would doing this violate any _____?
- Have I actually calculated the _____ over time and compared the answer to other avenues?
- Do I have _____ about this?

How do you go about getting a spirit of peace?

_____

_____

_____

_____

_____

As the simplest of summaries, good stewardship requires three things:

- Apply good math to the facts, especially when it comes to debt. Like the prudent king and builder in Jesus' parable, you must count both the short-term and long-term costs.
- Evaluate your heart. Examine your motives with brutal honesty. Avoid the inclination to rationalize any desire.
- Check with God. Pray and ask for guidance from the Spirit. Speak with an accountability partner. Look at God's Word. Make sure that you have *peace* before you move forward.

Good stewardship, including a proper approach to debt, applies to organizations as well as to individuals and families. Read the account of Gateway Church's decision to evaluate its finances and accelerate its debt payments. What principles do you see at work here? How can you apply those principles in your thinking about personal debt? Also, if you happen to own a business, how might you apply those principles in your business finances?

_____

_____

_____

_____

Key Quotes:

"I'm not against *all* debt in *all* circumstances."

"Wise stewards get blessed, and blessed people can be lenders, sharers, and generous givers."

"Do whatever is necessary for as long as necessary to get out from under the burden of debt."

"My point is good stewardship requires good math—especially when considering acquiring debt."

"Debt is a dangerous tool. Use it sparingly, prudently, and prayerfully."

CHAPTER FIFTEEN

BLESSED TO BE A BLESSING

Consider this Scripture:

> I planted, Apollos watered, but God gave the increase. So then neither he who plants is anything, nor he who waters, but God who gives the increase. Now he who plants and he who waters are one, and each one will receive his own reward according to his own labor (1 Corinthians 3:6–8).

In these chapters we've explored many aspects of stewardship. We've seen several examples of how God has used His faithful servants to further His kingdom's purposes with their resources.

We talked earlier about how our perspective and expectations impact our approach to stewardship. How does Paul describe what our perspective should be in verse 7? What does Paul say about our expectations in verse 8?

_____

_____

_____

Mitch and Mandy are another example of achieving stewardship and all its benefits.

Read Psalm 24:1. What fundamental principle of stewardship did this Scripture impress upon Mitch? What is the difference between an owner and a steward?

_____

_____

_____

_____

Read 1 Corinthians 4:2. What does this verse say about how God measures the quality of our stewardship? How did Mitch and Mandy start on the road to becoming faithful stewards?

Once they achieved their initial goal of getting their financial lives in order, much of the stress, fear, and worry that had been a part of their married life for ten years vanished. They were then able to truly have fun by being able to consistently bless others. Beyond that, there is even more.

> For the Jews it was a time of happiness and joy, gladness and honor. (Esther 8:16 NIV)

> Give your father and mother joy! May she who gave you birth be happy. (Proverbs 23:25 NLT)

The Greek word translated as "blessed" in the New Testament literally means "happy." The life of a faithful steward is a "blessed life." But that life is a means to an end: a life of joy.

Read Luke 16:9–13 again. Jesus explains how "unrighteous mammon" can be used to righteous ends by sharing the good news with others.

Hebrews 12:2 says that Jesus endured the cross "for the joy that was set before Him." What was that joy? The restoration of all creation and the salvation of God's elect through His Church.

Read Philippians 3. In this chapter, Paul summarizes the life and goal of the believer. What does Paul tell the brethren to do at the beginning of verse 1? What is Paul "reaching for" in verse 14?

_____

_____

_____

_____

Now, read Philippians 4:1. What does Paul mean when he describes the believers there as "my beloved and longed-for brethren, my *joy* and crown" (emphasis added)?

_____

_____

_____

_____

Good stewardship provides the blessing—the happiness—that God wants us to use to bless others and bring salvation and the kingdom of God to other people. After all, the Church is all about people. Paul's joy and crown are those he led to the Lord.

According to the text, as you walk down Stewardship Road, what are the four things that comprise the basis of stewardship?

_____

_____

_____

_____

What were the words my daughter said when I confessed that I was the man who gave away $100 bills?

_____

_____

_____

_____

Wise stewardship impacts past, present, and future. You can heal mistakes of the past, find peace and happiness in the present, and create a lasting legacy that extends beyond your time on earth. You can pursue a lifestyle of generosity. What a joy it would be to hear every believer's child say, "I want to be just like you, Daddy!"

Paul said much the same thing in Philippians 3:10: "That I may know Him and the power of His resurrection, and the fellowship of His sufferings, being conformed to His death."

In other words: "I want to be just like you, Daddy!"

John records a similar sentiment in John 5:19: "Then Jesus answered and said to them, 'Most assuredly, I say to you, the Son can do nothing of Himself, but what He sees the Father do; *for whatever He does, the Son also does in like manner.*'" (emphasis added). Jesus *was* (and is) just like His Daddy!

When you are known to be just like your Daddy, you will create a lasting legacy that extends far beyond your brief time on this earth. That's powerful!

Key Quotes:

"The quality of our stewardship is measured in terms of 'faithfulness.'"

"What's better than happiness? Joy.... Happiness is great, but deep joy is even better."

"Your wise stewardship creates a lasting legacy that extends far beyond your brief time on this earth. It's that powerful."

NOTES

1. The CIA World Factbook. Accessed September 30, 2018, https://www.cia.gov/library/publications/the-world-factbook/geos/ao.html.

2. The CIA World Factbook. Accessed September 30, 2018, https://www.cia.gov/library/publications/resources/the-world-factbook/geos/us.html.

3. "United States Consumer Spending 1950–2018," *Trading Economics*. Accessed September 30, 2018, https://tradingeconomics.com/united-states/consumer-spending.

4. Bureau of Economic Analysis, Personal Income and Outlays, July 2018. Accessed September 30, 2018, https://www.bea.gov/news/2018/personal-income-and-outlays-july-2018.

5. Josh Mitchell, "U.S. Consumer Spending Rose 0.4% in July," *Wall Street Journal*, August 30, 2018. Accessed September 30, 2018, https://www.wsj.com/articles/u-s-consumer-spending-rose-0-4-in-july-1535632480.

6. Evan Halper, "Trump tax cuts carry a big price tag: Huge debt and risk of another financial crisis, budget office warns," *LA Times*. Accessed September 30, 2018, http://www.latimes.com/politics/la-na-pol-tax-cuts-debt-20180626-story.html.

7. Jill Barshay, "U.S. now ranks near the bottom among 35 industrialized nations in math," The Hechinger Report, December 6, 2016. Accessed September 30, 2018, https://hechingerreport.org/u-s-now-ranks-near-bottom-among-35-industrialized-nations-math/.

8. Tara Lachapelle, "Lessons Learned From the Downfall of Toys 'R' Us," *Bloomberg Businessweek*, March 9, 2018. Accessed September 30, 2018, https://www.bloomberg.com/news/articles/2018-03-09/toys-r-us-downfall-is-ominous-reminder-about-debt-laden-deals.

ABOUT THE AUTHOR

ROBERT MORRIS is the lead senior pastor of Gateway Church, a multicampus church in the Dallas–Fort Worth Metroplex. Since it began in 2000, the church has grown to more than 39,000 active members. His television program is aired in over 190 countries, and his radio feature, *Worship & the Word with Pastor Robert*, airs on radio stations across America. He serves as chancellor of The King's University and is the bestselling author of numerous books, including *The Blessed Life*, *The God I Never Knew*, *Truly Free*, and *Frequency*. Robert and his wife, Debbie, have been married thirty-eight years and are blessed with one married daughter, two married sons, and nine grandchildren.